101 DIGITAL
PHOTO TIPs

NICK VANDOME

in
easy steps

In easy steps is an imprint of Computer Step
Southfield Road · Southam
Warwickshire CV47 0FB · United Kingdom
www.ineasysteps.com

Notice of Liability
Every effort has been made to ensure that this book contains accurate and current information. However, Computer Step and the author shall not be liable for any loss or damage suffered by readers as a result of any information contained herein.

Trademarks
All trademarks are acknowledged as belonging to their respective companies.

Printed and bound in the United Kingdom

ISBN 1-84078-308-7

TABLE OF CONTENTS

EXPOSURE AND METERING 57

PEOPLE 79

ARCHITECTURE 95

LANDSCAPES 115

MOTION 135

COMPOSITION 147

INDEX 187

BEFORE YOU START

It is obvious that the best thing about a digital camera is taking pictures. However, before you start snapping away there are some basic technical issues that should be looked at and understood. This section offers some tips covering these issues so that you can start taking better pictures with your camera.

Covers

Know your camera

When you first get your hands on a digital camera, whether it is a new one or an upgrade to an existing model, the temptation is to rush off and start taking pictures as soon as possible. While this is a natural reaction, and it does no harm to take a few shots as soon as the camera is out of the box, you will benefit greatly in the long run if you take a bit of time to get to know your camera and its functions.

The first place to start in becoming familiar with your camera is the dreaded manual. These are invariably not the easiest things to read but they can play a vital role in understanding the technical capabilities of your camera. Once you have taken your first few shots, it is well worth settling down with the manual for an hour or so, to get the maximum functionality out of your camera.

Most digital cameras also come with a Quick Start guide. This covers information such as inserting the battery and the camera's memory card, and shows how to turn on the camera and take your first shots.

It is well worth settling down with the manual for an hour or so

Some of the areas in which the manual can be useful are for setting the image resolution (i.e. the size at which images are captured), using the various specialized modes (see next Tip), and altering camera settings such as white balance and film speed (ISO) equivalent settings. It can also be used to access what can seem like simple functions – but only if you know how – such as activating the camera's flash or recording video.

The manual can also be used to find out how to access the camera's menus and then make the relevant selections. This can help you set up your camera for particular types of shots and also give you the knowledge and confidence to change settings quickly and efficiently. When you are taking photographs this can make the difference between capturing the perfect shot and just missing it because you are still fiddling around with the camera.

Once you have read through the manual, take some experimental shots to use the various functions that you have learned about. Remember, you are not wasting any film so take your time to see how the different settings on your camera work and how the resultant images compare with each other.

② Using scene modes

igital cameras have come a long way in a very short period of time and now even the entry-level models contain a good selection of options for how the camera functions. These include traditional camera settings such as aperture or shutter speed priority (see next Tip) and also preset modes. These are becoming increasingly common and it is certainly worth looking for a digital camera that has at least half a dozen of these modes.

Camera preset modes are designed to simplify the operation of capturing images in certain conditions or for certain effects. For instance, if you want to capture a portrait with a blurred background to make the main subject more prominent this can be achieved by adjusting the depth of field with the camera's aperture control. Alternatively, you could just select the Portrait mode and the camera will choose all of the appropriate settings for you. Even so, it is still worthwhile trying to understand why certain settings are being selected for certain modes.

When a camera mode is used, the selections made by the camera are displayed in the viewfinder or the LCD panel. If you look at these then you will get some idea of the way the shot is being captured. In time, you should be able to apply these settings yourself for particular shooting conditions.

Camera modes can usually be selected from within the camera's menu system (which is another reason why it is a good idea to consult the camera's manual) and it is also possible to specify a certain mode in which the camera will start up. However, this can be a risky option as you may want to capture a different type of image when you next turn on the camera for use.

Camera modes are an excellent option for gaining confidence in capturing images in a variety of shooting conditions.

For some camera modes, such as those used at night or in low-level lighting conditions, the selections may mean that the camera is using a slow shutter speed. This means that the camera's shutter is open for a longer period of time while the shot is being captured. If this is slower than 1/60th second then a tripod should be used to keep the camera steady.

MODES

Some common modes include:

- Portrait
- Sport
- Landscape
- Close-up
- Fireworks
- Snow
- Backlight

9

Aperture and shutter speed

Two of the most common terms used by photographers are aperture priority and shutter speed priority. These are two camera settings that enable you to assert a certain degree of control over how the shot is going to be captured. Traditionally, aperture and shutter speed controls were only available on more sophisticated, high-end cameras. However, an increasing range of digital cameras are now available with this functionality and it is possible for anyone to make the most of the techniques that these options afford. On most cameras, aperture priority is denoted by an A on the camera's menu or a dial on the camera body, while shutter speed priority is denoted by an S. The combination of the aperture settings and the shutter speed determines how much light enters the camera when a shot is taken and ultimately affects the exposure of the image.

For more tips and information about aperture priority and depth of field, see Exposure and Metering.

The aperture of a camera is a diaphragm within the lens. This has a certain diameter that allows differing amounts of light into the camera. The size of the aperture can be changed to alter the amount of light entering the camera. This can either be done automatically by the camera or it can be done by the photographer, which is what happens when the camera is in aperture priority mode. The size of the aperture also affects another photographic technique, known as depth of field. This determines how much of an image is within the area of focus. If the aperture is at its widest then the depth of field is smaller, which means less of the image will be in focus in front of and behind the main subject. If the aperture is at its narrowest then the depth of field is greater, which means more of the image is in focus. Aperture priority can be used to create effects such as the blurred background in the top image on the facing page, which was achieved with a wide aperture.

For more tips and information about shutter speed priority, see the section on Motion.

A camera's shutter is the set of blades that open and close when the shutter release button is pressed and a photograph is taken. The time that the shutter remains open affects how much light enters the camera. In shutter priority mode the speed at which the shutter opens and closes can be set according to the type of shot being captured. For instance, if you are trying to capture an image of a sporting event you will need a very fast shutter speed in order to freeze the action. Conversely, if you want to created a blurred image for effect, then a slow shutter speed can be used. This is particularly effective when capturing images of water. The bottom image on the facing page was captured with a slow shutter speed and the camera on a tripod to create an effective sense of motion.

Getting to grips with exposure

Exposure is a vital part of photography and refers to the overall amount of light that enters the camera. This is controlled by a combination of the aperture and shutter speed settings. If fully automatic mode is selected on a camera – i.e. no manual settings are applied – then the camera will view a shot and assess how much light is needed to expose it correctly. This means that the final image should not look too dark or too light. When assessing the exposure, the camera will set the aperture size and then select a shutter speed that will enable enough light to pass through the aperture. Aperture settings are known as f-stops (or f-numbers) and shutter speeds are measured in seconds or fractions of a second.

A wide aperture has a low f-number, e.g. f2.8, while a narrow aperture has a high f-number, e.g. f22.

If you want to take more control over your images you can use aperture priority or shutter speed priority. This means that you set either the aperture or shutter speed and then the camera will select the appropriate setting for the other. However, the combination still has to allow enough light to enter the camera for the shot to be exposed correctly. For instance, if you want a very fast shutter speed (such as for a sporting event) then the camera will probably select a wide aperture setting so that more light can enter the camera over the short period of time during which the shutter will be open. Conversely, if you want to select a very narrow aperture (to capture a large depth of field, i.e. a large area in focus) the camera will probably select a slower shutter speed to allow more time for the light to pass through the narrow aperture.

A lot of digital cameras will indicate if a shot is going to be over- or under-exposed before it is taken. If it is going to be over-exposed then reduce the amount of light by narrowing the aperture or increasing the shutter speed. If it is going to be under-exposed, increase the amount of light by increasing the aperture or reducing the shutter speed.

SETTINGS

Some combinations of aperture and shutter speed that should produce well-exposed images on a sunny day:

- f5.6 at 1/500th sec
- f8 at 1/250th sec
- f11 at 1/125th sec
- f16 at 1/60th sec

The images on the facing page show the results of mistakes with the exposure settings. The top image was taken with a wide aperture but the shutter speed was too slow so too much light entered the camera leading to an over-exposed image. The middle image was taken with the correct shutter speed but the aperture was too narrow so that there is not enough light and it is therefore under-exposed. The bottom image is correctly exposed.

For most shooting conditions there are usually at least four combinations of aperture and shutter speed that can be used. Which one is selected will be determined by the type of shot you want: i.e. one with a small or large depth of field.

5 Fathoming focal length

The term focal length is another piece of photography jargon that is worth getting to know about. It refers to the distance between the camera's lens and the point at which the image is in focus within the lens. Focal length is measured in millimeters, e.g. 105mm.

For the majority of digital camera users, the issue of focal length is closely linked with the idea of being able to zoom in and out of an image. A lot of digital cameras now have optical zoom facilities, which means the focal length of the lens can be altered so that the main subject appears closer or further away. This is done by physically changing the distance between the camera's lens and the focused image. In general you should look for a camera with an optical zoom of approximately 5x. However, do not be taken in by the digital zoom figures that are advertised with digital cameras. This is just a device that increases the size of an image in the viewfinder or LCD panel and results in an inferior quality image as the individual pixels are just made to look bigger.

> ## Do not be taken in by digital zoom figures

Due to the architecture of digital cameras the quoted size of a zoom lens is the equivalent of 1.5 to 4 times larger than that of a zoom lens on a 35mm film camera. So a 9mm to 70mm zoom lens on a digital camera could be equivalent to 35mm to 280mm (approximately) on a film camera.

The focal length of a camera's lens is important for two main reasons. Firstly, the greater the focal length, the closer you can make a subject appear. This is particularly useful if it is a zoom lens, i.e. a lens with a varying focal length. This means that differing shots can be captured from a similar position. In the examples on the facing page, the top image was taken with a short focal length while the bottom one was taken with a larger focal length. This provides two different images by simply changing the focal length of the lens on the camera.

Zoom lenses on compact digital cameras are frequently quoted as multiples, e.g. 2x, 5x or 12x.

The second reason that focal length is important is to do with depth of field: as you zoom in on an image (increase the focal length) the depth of field decreases: i.e. less of the image is in focus behind and in front of the main subject. This can be particularly useful for portrait shots. With a zoom lens you can take a portrait shot without getting too close to the subject and the large focal length of the zoom will help ensure that the background behind the main subject has a pleasant blurred effect. This will soften the image and create an effective portrait.

BEFORE YOU START

14

15

Spot-on focusing

A uto-focus is now a common feature in digital cameras. It is operated by half-depressing and holding the shutter release button. The camera then focuses on the subject in the middle of the viewfinder and once this is done a solid light appears to alert you to the fact that the image is in focus. The shutter release button can then be fully depressed to capture the image. However, despite this apparent ease of use, there are still some issues that have to be considered to get the most out of auto-focus.

The first problem with auto-focus can occur when capturing images in low-level lighting conditions. Auto-focus works by sensing the contrast between dark and light areas in an image, and if the overall image is too dark there will not be enough contrast to operate the auto-focus. One way to overcome this is to try and find an area of greater contrast in the scene, focus on this, and then move the camera back to the original shot. Alternatively, carry a piece of black and white striped card with you and place this in the middle of the shot. Use this to focus on the main subject (make sure the card is positioned at the required point of focus) and then take the shot.

Carry a piece of black and white striped card

Generally, more sophisticated focusing systems are available on more expensive digital cameras such as digital SLR (DSLR) cameras.

Another difficulty with for auto-focus is seen when capturing fast-moving objects. There are various techniques for achieving this (see Tips 72 and 73) but the first issue is to get point of focus right. One way to do this is to identify a spot where the moving object will be passing and focus on this. Then, when the object arrives at the selected point, the image can be captured.

When using a camera on a tripod and a slow shutter speed, use the self-timer option to trigger the shutter release. This will ensure that the camera is not shaken when the shutter release button is pressed.

One concept to be aware of when focusing on objects is that of camera shake. This is the blurred effect that can occur when the shutter speed is too slow for a particular shot. This is usually in the range of 1/60th second or slower. At times like this you should use a tripod, or use flash to add more light to the scene so that a faster shutter speed can be used. In the top image on the facing page the shot was taken without a tripod and because the level of light was fairly low the shutter speed had to be 1/15th second, resulting in the blurred image (even though it was focused correctly). In the bottom image, the camera was mounted on a tripod so that it remained steady while the shot was captured at the same settings.

17

Solving the resolution riddle

In the world of digital photography you will sooner or later (probably sooner) come across the concept of resolution. While it covers a number of aspects of digital photography, the most important one relates to the size of images in terms of pixels (the colored electronic building blocks that make up digital images). This can either be given as an overall headline figure, e.g. 8 million pixels, or 8 megapixels, or as the dimensions of an image, e.g. 1200 pixels x 900 pixels. The importance of pixels and resolution is that they determine the size at which images can be displayed and printed to a high quality.

Most digital cameras can capture images at different resolutions (with different numbers of pixels) and, as a general rule, for printed images you want as many pixels as possible, while for images that are going to be displayed online a much lower resolution can be used. For printed images a setting of 300 pixels per inch (ppi) is used for optimum quality. This means that 300 pixels will be placed in each linear inch of the printed image.

The resolution of an image can be changed in an image editing program such as Photoshop Elements, Paint Shop Pro or Ulead Express.

For printed images you want as many pixels as possible

To work out the size of the final printed image, divide the pixel dimensions of the image by 300. So an image with a resolution of 1200 x 900 would be able to be printed at 4 inches x 3 inches at high quality. The following table illustrates the resolution, in terms of number of pixels, required for certain sizes of print (presuming that they are printed at 300 ppi).

OVERALL PIXELS	DIMENSIONS (pixels)	PRINT SIZE (inches at 300 ppi)
8 million	3264 x 2448	11 x 8 (approx.)
5 million	2592 x 1944	8 x 6 (approx.)
3 million	2048 x 1536	7 x 5 (approx.)
1 million	1280 x 960	4 x 3 (approx.)

Images on the Web are traditionally displayed at about 72 ppi as this is the resolution of standard computer monitors. Images can also be printed at a much lower setting than 300 ppi, but the quality deteriorates. The top image on the facing page was printed at 72 ppi while the one on the bottom was printed at 300 ppi, giving a much higher quality.

Reducing time lag

Every technology has its own individual quirks or drawbacks and in the case of digital photography one of these is time lag. This refers to the amount of time it takes the camera to turn on, the time lag between when the shot is taken and when it is actually captured and the time it takes for the camera to recycle a shot and then be ready for the next one. Of these three, there is a limited amount that you can do about the first two, except to get to know your camera as thoroughly as possible and then work with it accordingly.

Time lag when capturing a shot is not only frustrating; it can also ruin what could have been a great photo. There is usually a very brief pause between when the camera's shutter release button is pressed and when the camera captures the image. This is because there is a certain amount of digital wizardry that the camera has to perform before it can successfully capture an image. This may only cause a time lag of a few hundredths of a second, but this can make all the difference in an action shot, or a portrait shot, particularly with children.

Time lag can ruin what could have been a great photo

To try and reduce time lag the best option is to apply manual settings for options that the camera would otherwise set automatically. This includes the white balance and focusing – try pre-focusing on a subject and keeping the shutter release button half held down until you want to capture the shot. Another option is to use continuous shooting mode. This enables you to take several shots consecutively.

Most camera manuals or specification sheets list the actual time lag for capturing images. If all else fails, get to know your camera and try and compensate for the time lag. To a certain extent, it is a case of practice makes perfect.

TYPES OF TIME LAG

Start-up time lag. The amount of time between the camera being turned on and being ready for use.

Shot-time lag. The amount of time between pressing the shutter release and the actual taking of the picture.

Recycling time lag. The amount of time it takes to get ready for the next shot.

CAMERA TECHNIQUES

In many respects, digital cameras behave in a very similar way to film ones. This section gives some tips about simple camera techniques that can be deployed to improve the process of capturing images.

Covers

Camera orientation

Taking good photographs does not have to involve large amounts of high-tech, expensive equipment. In a lot of cases a good eye for a photograph can be more important than the equipment being used. Part of this involves changing the angle at which an image is being viewed. There are a number of ways in which this can be achieved, but the simplest is to change the camera's orientation. This is a case of rotating the camera by 90 degrees so that the image is captured in portrait rather than landscape.

A good eye for a photograph can be more important than the equipment being used

Even if you have taken one good photograph, this simple technique of changing the orientation can ensure that you have another impressive shot, which shows the subject from a different perspective. Since you are not using up any film it is always worthwhile to take shots with different orientations so that you can compare them at a later date. Also, if you want to crop the image (see next Tip) you will have more scope to do this if you have the main subject in different orientations.

TILTING

Another option for changing the orientation is rotating the camera to an angle rather than holding it horizontal or vertical. This can be particularly effective with landscape shots to emphasize angles. However, it is an effect that should be used as an extra option once more conventional shots have been taken.

With the examples on the facing page the top image is captured in landscape orientation, which gives the opportunity to highlight the concentration of yacht masts and their density. The bottom image is in portrait mode, which allows for the scene to be expanded and includes more of the foreground, giving it greater context. This shows how differing images can be captured from the same spot simply by changing the orientation of the camera.

10 Cropping and image size

As shown in Tip 7, the physical size of an image is an important factor in assessing the quality and size of printed images. For images straight out of the camera this is a fairly simple calculation: the pixel dimensions of the image divided by 300 (the optimum setting for printing images). However, if you want to edit images then this may have an impact on the pixel dimensions. This is particularly true if the image is going to be cropped, one of the most popular image editing techniques and one that can be done with image editing software or within photo kiosks at photography printing outlets.

Cropping involves removing unwanted areas from an image. This is usually done by selecting the area you want to keep (as a rectangle within the image) and then discarding the rest of the image. See the two examples on the facing page. Obviously, this has an impact on the pixel dimensions of the image as some of the original pixels in the image have been discarded.

The resolution of images when they are printed can be greater than 300 pixels per inch, but try not to let it fall too far below this.

If you are cropping an image it is important to make sure that the edited image is still large enough to be printed at a good quality at the required size. To check this, divide the pixel dimensions of the cropped image by 300. So for example if you want to print at 7 inches by 5 inches then the edited image will need to be approximately 2100 pixels by 1500 pixels, or more.

The issue of cropping and image size is one of the reasons why it is always valuable to capture images at the maximum resolution: you do not always know how much you will want to keep or remove in an image but with the highest resolution available you will have a lot more flexibility if you want to edit your images.

FRAME FILLING

In some instances it is advisable to fill the frame with as much of the subject as possible (see Tip 44). However, if you think you will want to crop an image it is better to leave some extra room around the subject when the image is captured. Then, as long as the resolution is large enough, the final image can be cropped and printed to a high enough quality.

Be safe with bracketing

One of the problems with film photography is that you never really know how an image is going to look until it is printed. With digital cameras this drawback is largely removed by the facility to review images with the LCD panel as soon as they have been taken. However, LCD panels do not always give a totally accurate depiction of the color and exposure of an image and it can sometimes be difficult to see the image clearly, particularly if there is sun or direct light shining on the LCD. In order to make sure you capture a perfectly exposed shot, the technique of bracketing can be used.

Bracketing is a photographic technique that involves capturing an image for a range of exposure settings. This means that at least one of the shots should be correctly exposed. To use bracketing, a camera has to have an option for exposure

Bracketing ensures that an image is captured for a range of exposure settings

compensation (check your camera's manual for details).

Check your camera's manual to see if it has exposure compensation.
For more information on this, see Exposure and Metering.

To use bracketing, capture an image in any shooting mode, e.g. automatic, aperture priority, shutter speed priority or fully manual. Then select an exposure compensation value (see Tip 34 for more details about exposure compensation) to make the image either darker or lighter. To make an image lighter select a positive exposure compensation value and to make it darker use a negative value. For bracketing, use at least one example above and one below the settings for the initial shot. Remember, images sometimes look slightly different on a computer as opposed to the camera's LCD panel.

BETTER SAFE

Bracketing is especially important for locations that you may not be visiting again. The middle image on the facing page is correctly exposed, but two more were captured using +/−1 exposure compensation, in case these images were an improvement.

Capturing macro shots

Macro photography is another term for close-up shots. These types of shot take advantage of a camera's ability to capture images at very close distances. Most digital cameras have a macro mode that enables them to focus on subjects at very close distances, up to a few centimeters in some cases.

One of the main issues with macro shots is focusing. This is because the focusing has to be very accurate at such a close distance as there is little margin for error. One problem is that the object has to be very still for the auto-focus to work, so if there is even slight movement this will be magnified greatly as far as the focusing is concerned. So if you are taking photos of subjects such as flowers or insects try and do so when there is very little wind, or use some form of wind break to ensure that the subject is as still as possible.

Macro shots can also cause problems with focusing if there is not enough contrast within the shot – since you will be focusing on one small area of an object there may not be enough contrast within that area. If this is the case try finding an edge within the subject (this may involve moving the camera, focusing and then recomposing the shot while still keeping the shutter release button held down to retain focus) but make sure it is at the same distance as the intended subject. Another option is to use a black and white striped card and hold this at the point of focus within the image.

Another issue is that close-up shots have a very narrow depth of field, i.e. very little of the object is in focus. This means that you have to focus very accurately to make sure the correct part of the image is in focus. In the image on the facing page the center of the image is in focus, while the background is blurred due to the very small depth of field.

Macro mode is usually accessed from a button or a dial on the camera's body. In some cases it may be on one of the camera's menus. Macro mode is usually denoted by a tulip symbol.

Check your camera's manual to find the exact range for the macro function.

> ## BACKGROUNDS
>
> Be careful with backgrounds in macros shots to ensure they do not detract from the main subject. One way to do this is to have a wide aperture (e.g. f2.8, f4 or f5) so that the depth of field is very small, and the background becomes blurred so as not to be a distraction.

Zooming effectively

A digital SLR (Single Lens Reflex) camera is one that has detachable lenses that fit onto the camera body. They are generally more expensive than compact digital cameras but offer more functions.

For a camera with a zoom lens, either a fixed zoom lens or one fitted to a digital SLR camera, it is always worthwhile to experiment with the zoom function for particular shots. In some cases the wide angle shot may be more effective, while in others the zoomed version will be better. In an ideal situation, both versions of the image will stand up in their own right.

When working with zoom it is important to use it creatively, not just presume that a zoomed version of a wide angle shot will work well. In some cases it will, while in others it may take a little more work to get the best picture.

When using zoom, the first option is to capture the same shot at different focal lengths, i.e. with varying amounts of zoom applied. Start with the zoom at its widest angle, i.e. fully retracted, and then retake the picture as you zoom in closer and closer. This should provide a good range of shots of the same image, but some will be more effective than others.

Take the zoomed shot from a different viewpoint

Another way to use the zoom is to take a wide angled shot and then focus on a particular aspect of a subject with the zoom. This could mean that you take the zoomed shot from a different viewpoint, as with the two images on the facing page. The top image is a standard wide angle shot of the subject. A closer version could have also been taken with the zoom from the same position, but instead the angle of shooting was changed so that the zoomed image is of another part of the main subject. Taken together, the two images manage to convey both the structure and the character of the church.

WATCH THE BORDER

When capturing shots at the highest zoom setting it is worthwhile leaving a small border between the subject and the outside of the image. This will allow for the image to be cropped slightly during the printing process if necessary.

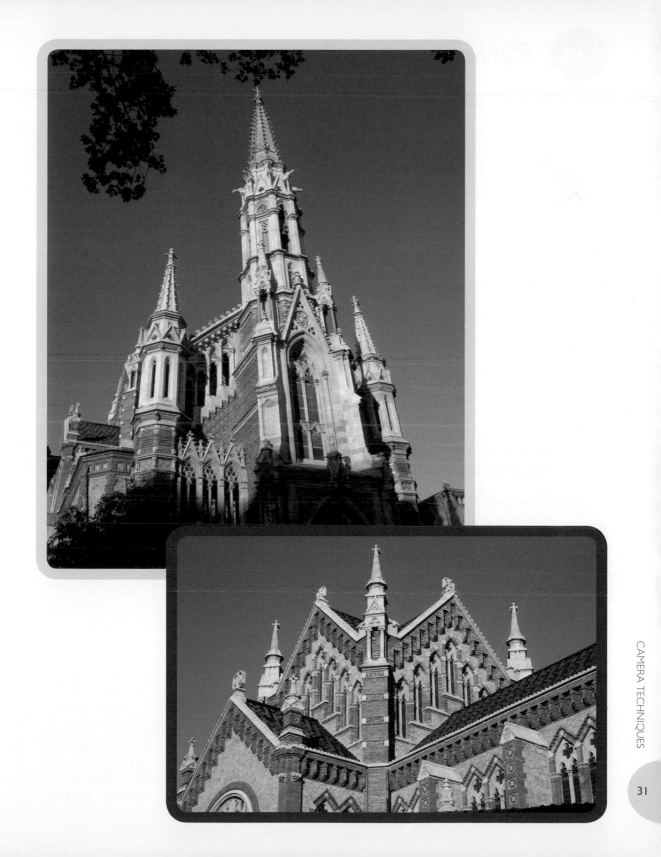

Perfecting parallax

One of the problems with compact digital cameras is that some types of viewfinders do not see exactly the same area of the image as that captured on the sensor. This is the case with optical viewfinders, which look at the subject from a slightly different angle than the lens of the camera does. At medium and long distances this is not a problem, as the difference is relatively small and is not noticeable over distances of a few feet. However, problems can occur when you are trying to capture close-up images: while the subject appears in the center of the viewfinder it is slightly off-center when the shot is captured (see the top image on the facing page). This is known as parallax and there are a number of ways to try and overcome it.

Some digital cameras have an option for alternating between the viewfinder and the LCD panel for framing shots. Use the viewfinder option if you want to conserve your batteries and the LCD panel to get well-framed close-ups.

The first way to overcome the problem of parallax is to use the camera's LCD display for framing the image. Most digital cameras have these types of displays at the back of the camera body and they show you exactly what is seen through the lens of the camera. The drawbacks with using the LCD panel in this way are that it uses up comparatively more battery power than an optical viewfinder and it can be hard to see the image within the panel in strong light such as bright sunlight.

Use the camera's LCD display for framing the image

Digital SLR cameras do not suffer from parallax. What you see through the viewfinder is how the final image will appear.

Another way of avoiding parallax problems is available if the viewfinder has correction marks visible within it. These are vertical and horizontal lines within the viewfinder that show the actual area of the subject that is going to be captured. By lining up the subject with the correction marks it should be possible to frame the image accurately. When viewing an image with correction marks it will probably appear off-center, but if you have framed it correctly within the marks the final image should be centered. The bottom image on the facing page was captured using the correction marks within the viewfinder.

Instead of optical viewfinders, some digital cameras now have electronic TTL (Through The Lens) viewfinders. These use a combination of mirrors within the camera to accurately represent what is being seen through the lens. TTL viewfinders tend to be more accurate than optical ones for displaying the correct position of close-up objects.

Keeping the camera steady

For certain types of shots it is vital to keep the camera as steady as possible. This is because if the shutter speed falls below about 1/60th second then the camera will move slightly as the shot is being captured. This can result in a slightly blurred image caused by what is known as "camera shake".

The best way to keep the camera steady and avoid camera shake is to use a tripod. These come in a variety of sizes and weights but even a small, lightweight one will greatly assist in keeping the camera still while the shot is being taken. Get into the habit of taking a tripod with you whenever you are using your camera as you never know when you might need to take a shot with a slow shutter speed.

Get into the habit of taking a tripod with you whenever you are using your camera

The slower the shutter speed the more chance there is for camera shake.

In some cases, even the pressing of the shutter release button when a camera is on a tripod can cause slight camera shake. To remove the risk of this, the self-timer option can be used so that the camera fires automatically after a certain period of time once the timer has been activated. Alternatively, some cameras have cable releases or infrared remote controls that can be used to take the shot.

STEADY AS IT GOES

Conditions that will require extra support include:

• Night shots

• Indoor shots

• Slow shutter speeds to create a blurred effect for motion

• A camera with a large telephoto lens

If you do not have a tripod a good alternative is to rest the camera on a cushion. It is worthwhile carrying a small cushion, or bean-bag, around with you when you are taking pictures so that you can always have a steady platform for your camera. If all else fails, try supporting your camera against a bench or a door-frame.

LIGHTING

Light is a vital component for all photography. This section reveals various tips about how to find the best light and how to capture shots in a variety of lighting conditions.

Covers

Indoor shots

Light is one of the essential ingredients for any photograph but this does not mean that you have to have bright sunlight to capture a good image. Indeed, with a bit of planning and experience it is possible to take good pictures in any lighting conditions.

One area about which people are sometimes unsure is taking pictures indoors. In a lot of cases this will result in the photographer immediately activating the flash on the camera. Sometimes this will work, but only if the subject is within range of the flash. However, for a large indoor area, such as the interior of a church, the flash will be ineffective; it will light up a small area in the foreground while the rest of the image will look too dark. Instead of using the flash a more versatile implement for indoor photography is a tripod. This will enable you to use a slow shutter speed on the camera, thus allowing enough light to enter the camera to capture a well-lit scene without the need for flash.

When capturing images indoors without the flash the use of a tripod is essential to keep the camera still for a slow shutter speed. If the camera were to be hand-held then the image would end up looking blurred due to camera shake. Make sure you have a sturdy tripod and pay particular attention to the tripod head on which the camera is mounted. This should be as steady as possible. Once the tripod is set up, set the camera to aperture priority mode and select an aperture for the type of shot you want to capture (a wide aperture for a small area in focus and a narrow aperture for a large area in focus). The camera will then select a suitable shutter speed, which may be well over a second. If possible, use the camera's self-timer or a shutter release cable to trip the shutter release as this will reduce further the chance of camera shake.

The top image on the facing page was taken with a wide aperture (f4.2) and a shutter speed of 1/8th second. Due to the amount of light from the candles this was enough to illuminate the scene and give it a very evocative feel. In the bottom image on the facing page a high ISO value of 1600 was used to increase the camera's sensitivity to light. This meant that a faster shutter speed of 1/60th second could be used and so the camera could still be hand-held rather than put on a tripod. (See Tip 24 for more details about ISO values.)

Check your camera's manual to see the available range of ISO settings. Some cameras go up to 1600, while others may only go to 400. This can have a significant impact on capturing indoor shots as a higher ISO range may enable you to capture shots without the need for a tripod.

Shooting against the light

One standard photography rule is to ensure that you have the sun at your back when you are capturing images. This is known as front lighting, i.e. the light is falling on the front of the subject. While in general this is a good rule to follow there are times when breaking it can provide very effective images. Indeed, shooting against the light in this way can produce more creative images than the more conventional frontlit scenes.

When shooting against the light, some of the best results can be achieved when the sun, or main light source, is at least partially obscured by the main subject. Otherwise the sun may be too bright, resulting in lens glare in the image. However, shooting directly into the sun can produce dramatic results – but you have to be very careful with this type of shot, both from a creative point of view and also for your own welfare as it is not advisable to look directly into the sun through the viewfinder or the LCD panel. If the sun is partially obscured then it will become an integral part of the shot, as well as being the light source.

> **Some of the best results can be achieved when the sun is at least partially obscured by the main subject**

Do not look directly at the sun through either the camera's viewfinder or the LCD panel as this could seriously damage your eyes.

Usually when shooting against the light there is a considerable contrast between the light and the main subject as the light is a lot brighter than the subject. This can cause exposure problems and you may have to make a conscious decision about taking a light reading. Where you take a meter reading from depends on which area of the image you want to give most prominence to: either the main subject or the light source itself.

See Tip 20 for information about using the camera to take a light meter reading.

In the top image on the facing page the meter reading was taken from the sun to emphasize its size. This resulted in the main subject being under-exposed, thus creating the silhouette effect (for more on creating silhouettes see Tip 37). In the bottom image the metering was taken from the middle of the fountain so that the water was still visible and the light behind it created the dramatic effect.

Fill-in flash

Although front lighting is a common option for a variety of photographic situations it can have its disadvantages too. One of these is seen when capturing images of people. If the main subjects are lit from the front they may appear bright but the light inevitably causes them to squint, or shade their faces from the bright sunlight. This usually results in a very unnatural and strained-looking portrait.

One solution to this problem is to position the subjects with the sun behind them. This removes the strain on their eyes and allows them to look more relaxed. However, this causes its own problems as the back lighting results in their faces being in shadow. This is the case in the top image on the facing page, where the subjects look unnaturally shaded even though it is a bright, sunny day.

The solution to this problem lies in a technique known as fill-in flash. It may seem strange to use the flash when you are outside in the sun but this is the best way to ensure a well-balanced portrait when a subject is backlit by the sun. To achieve this, you have to actively turn on the flash to fire on every shot (if the camera is in automatic mode it

Fill-in flash can be used for any backlit subject, not just a portrait.

This is the best way to ensure a well-balanced portrait when a subject is backlit by the sun

will calculate that there is enough light in the scene without the need for flash). Once the flash has been activated it is just a case of taking the shot as normal. This is how the bottom image on the facing page was captured: the flash lights up the faces and this balances out the scene with the sunlit background. In some cases you may need to experiment with the distance between you and your subjects so that you get the correct amount of flash falling on their faces. (Consult your camera's manual to see the range of your flash.)

Another way to capture this type of image is to use a light source to the side of the subjects. This can produce the most sympathetic lighting effect and means that fill-in flash is not required.

Polarizing filters

The use of image editing programs means that a lot of special effects that were previously created using filters on cameras can now be done on computers. However, there is still a use for filters in some creative situations and there is one filter that should always be considered. This is a polarizing filter (or polarizer) and this is a filter that works in way that cannot be re-created on a computer.

Polarizing filters can be attached to the front of lenses on digital SLR cameras. If you want to use one on a compact digital camera you will need a lens attachment. This can be used on some types of compact camera and screws on around the lens. A polarizing filter can then be added to the attachment. However, on compact digital cameras the polarizing effect can only be seen once the shot has been taken. On a digital SLR camera the effect is visible as you turn the outer ring of the filter.

A polarizing filter operates by physically reducing the amount of glare in a scene created by vertical light. This allows for more prominence to be given to horizontal light in a scene. Polarizing filters are excellent for reducing glare from water and glass because of the way they block out light from certain angles. To do this, it is best to stand at an angle to the scene you are capturing (approximately 35 degrees) and then rotate the front ring on the polarizing filter until you see the glare start to disappear or reduce. The two images on the facing page show the difference when a polarizing filter is used to shoot through glass. The top one was captured without a filter and reveals a lot of glare. The bottom one used a polarizing filter to cut down the glare considerably.

Polarizing filters can also be used to improve the saturation and color of landscape shots, since they remove some of the unwanted vertical light in the scene. To do this, you have to be at approximately 90 degrees to the sun. It is therefore a useful option for capturing shots in the otherwise harsh midday sun. Since the sun is overhead, it is naturally at 90 degrees and you can use the polarizing filter to try and remove the harsh midday glare.

Polarizing filters are not cheap but they are a good investment if you are going to be taking a lot of landscape shots.

Polarizing filters do not usually cut out all of the glare from glass or water, but they can reduce it greatly.

Polarizing filters are excellent for reducing glare from water and glass

LIGHTING

Balancing varied lighting

One of the biggest problems for any photographer is capturing a correctly exposed image when there are wide variations in the lighting levels in a scene. Sometimes this can result in one area being too light (over-exposed), or too dark (under-exposed). Some of these issues are looked at in the section on Exposure and Metering. However, even in some scenes with very dark and very light areas it is still easy to capture a correctly exposed image. The secret is in looking at the scene and working out where the different areas of light are located.

The first thing to do when assessing the light in a scene is to know how your camera measures light. (It does this every time you capture an image, even if you are unaware that it is happening.) All digital cameras have an internal light meter which measures the amount of available light and, in automatic mode, adjusts the aperture and shutter speed so that the right amount of light is captured by the image sensor. This should result in a correctly exposed image most of the time

In the majority of cases the light meter within a digital camera will use a matrix method of measuring the available light. This works by looking at areas throughout the scene (generally at about 256 points) and then comparing this data with a database of lighting information taken from thousands of images captured in different lighting conditions. In the majority of cases the matrix method works very well. There are other methods of metering, such as spot metering and center-weighted metering, which are looked at in more detail in the Exposure and Metering section.

The image on the facing page looks as if it could cause problems for a camera's light meter because of the range of contrasting dark and light areas. However, since these are spread fairly evenly throughout the image the matrix metering method was able to cope well with it and set

METERING IN ACTION

To see how a camera's light meter works hold it up to different light sources and see how the exposure settings change for each of the light sources.

the correct exposure. Metering problems are more likely to occur when the dark and light parts of a scene are located in larger single areas, such as a very light sky and a dark foreground.

21 Reducing glare

As shown in Tip 17 it can sometimes be advantageous to shoot directly into the sun, mainly for creative and artistic purposes. However, one potential disadvantage of this is glare in the image from the bright sun. This is known as lens flare and although it can create some interesting effects, if it is overdone it can ruin an otherwise effective image.

The top image on the facing page suffers from too much glare. If there had been slightly less glare the shot might have worked but as it is the glare detracts too much from the image. Also, it makes the main subject look too watery since there is too much light in the scene, generated from the glare.

Luckily, with digital cameras it is possible to see if an image has too much glare in it, by viewing it through the LCD panel, and you can then act accordingly. One option is to accept that you will not be able to capture that particular shot at that moment, but there are also ways in which the image can still be saved.

One of the best options for consistently reducing glare and lens flare is to use a lens hood. This is a plastic attachment that fits on the front of the lens and shields the edges of the lens from light entering from unwanted angles. These are generally only available for detachable lenses for digital SLR cameras but there are now some attachments for compact digital cameras too.

Another, simpler option is to shade the lens with your free hand. Ideally, you should be able to block out the direct sunlight and then capture the shot. If you are trying this, make sure that your hand, or the shadow from it, does not appear in the image too.

A simpler option is to shade the lens with your free hand

Glare can also be reduced by physically moving slightly. You can still capture almost the same shot but if you turn to the side by a few degrees you may find that the glare is no longer visible in the viewfinder. Also, changing the camera orientation can help reduce glare. The bottom image on the facing page was captured after moving both the camera and the photographer, only slightly, but enough to remove the glare.

Glare can be used deliberately to create artistic effects in an image through the use of colored circles of light. However, use this sparingly and only after you have captured a conventional image.

Types of natural light

Since lighting is so important to photography, it is only natural that there is terminology for more than one type of light. These cover both daytime and night shooting, but in normal daytime conditions the main three types of light that interest the photographer are backlight, frontlight and sidelight.

Backlight occurs when the main source of light is behind a subject (as shown in Tip 17). This can cause problems for exposure (since the subject is in shadow while the background is brightly lit) but it also offers more creative opportunities. Once you learn how to set exposures for different parts of a scene you can use backlighting to create silhouettes or expose the main subject for an artistic effect. This can be particularly striking for macro (close-up) photography where the main subject is very small and is illuminated from behind.

Some digital cameras have a specific mode for dealing with backlight. This will usually fire the flash automatically to ensure the front of the subject is evenly lit against the bright background.

Frontlight is the opposite to backlight and occurs when the main source of light is behind the photographer and facing the subject. This creates a more even exposure but you have to be careful about the time of day when capturing frontlit subjects outside. If it is too near midday the sun will be too high in the sky. This will result in images that appear too harsh and with too much contrast: the sun at this time is at its brightest but this gives a "flat" light in photographic terms. (See Tip 23 for more details about capturing images during the Golden Hour.) In terms of lighting conditions for consistently good images, frontlight is the best bet. The two images on the facing page show the difference between a standard frontlit and backlit image. The top image is backlit: i.e. the sun is behind the main subject, leaving it in shade. The bottom image is frontlit, giving it a much better overall appearance since it is illuminated directly by the main light source.

EXPERIMENT

Capture the same subject at different times and in different lighting conditions, to see the effects this has on the image.

The other main type of lighting is sidelight. This is where the main light source is at the side of the subject. This is a particularly effective lighting source for portraits since it provides a good contrast on the subject's face: one side is brightly lit while the other is in shade. However, it is important to get the balance right or else the contrast between the two will be too great.

The Golden Hour

Great photography is not just about the direction and amount of light in an image. It is also about the quality of light. This is because light has differing qualities throughout the day, particularly sunlight: at midday the sun is at its strongest and, curiously, this is the worst time to capture images. Midday sun is too harsh and powerful and although it will produce a well-lit image the quality of the color will be lacking in depth and saturation. For the best photographs, the ideal lighting conditions usually occur approximately one hour after sunrise and one hour before sunset. In photographic terminology this is known as the Golden Hour.

The reason that the Golden Hour is so good for photography is because of the angle at which the light hits its subjects and because at these times it produces a deep glow rather than the harsh glare of midday sun. The morning and the evening Golden Hours produce slightly different effects: the morning sun has a soft golden effect while the evening sun tends to have a stronger orange glow with a bit more depth to it. Once you have experienced capturing images in the Golden Hour you will realize why it is so treasured by photographers (see image on facing page).

Make the effort to utilize the Golden Hour in your photography wherever you are. You will see a marked improvement in your images.

Although the Golden Hour can produce stunning photographic results it usually takes a bit more effort on the part of the photographer. In the morning you will have to be up and away before sunrise and in the evening you may not finish shooting until well into the evening. The essential thing is to make the most of these lighting opportunities when they present themselves. This may mean checking out a few shooting locations during normal daylight hours so you know exactly where to go when the Golden Hour occurs. You do not want to be wasting time finding locations when the light is at its best. A bit of forward planning can make all the difference when dealing with the Golden Hour.

The other thing to be aware of about the Golden Hour is that it is short. This means that you will not have a lot of time to move from location to location. It is best to pick a subject that you want to capture and then concentrate on a few top quality shots.

A final point about the Golden Hour is that it can produce great results in two directions. For instance, you may be looking at a fantastic sunset but if you turn around you may see a subject bathed in a glorious golden, orange light.

24 Creating grainy effects

As was shown in Tip 3, the aperture and shutter speed help determine the amount of light that can enter the camera for a particular shot. In addition to this, there is another function that can affect how light enters the camera. This is known as the ISO setting, or film speed in standard film photography terminology. A standard film speed is 100 or 200 for brightly lit conditions. Digital cameras have ISO equivalent ratings, usually in the range of 100–1600.

ISO speed refers to how quickly light is captured by the image sensor for a particular shot. If the ISO equivalent rating is 100 or 200 it means that the image sensor is less sensitive to light and so can capture images in bright conditions.

ISO speed refers to how quickly light is captured by the image sensor for a particular shot

However, a higher ISO rating means that the image sensor is more sensitive to light and so can capture images in more dimly lit conditions. Higher ISO ratings can be used for indoor shots or night shots.

In general, leave your camera on the default ISO equivalent rating which will probably be 100 or 200. This will deal with most normal daylight situations but remember that ISO ratings can be changed from shot to shot on a digital camera.

One option for ISO ratings is to create deliberately grainy effects in images. This is done by using a high ISO rating, such as 800 or 1600, which can create "noise" in an image. Noise is the speckled effect that is created by randomly distributed pixels within an image. With a high ISO setting the amount of noise increases and if it is created on purpose it is generally done for artistic purposes. The top image on the facing page was taken with an ISO rating of 1600. The bottom image was captured with an ISO rating of 200.

More expensive digital cameras, particularly digital SLR cameras, tend to create less noise than cheaper ones, even in low level lighting conditions.

By using a high ISO rating light is captured more quickly by the image sensor, so you can use a faster shutter speed. In some conditions, this can enable you to capture shots indoors or at night without the use of a tripod.

Dealing with white balance

Unfortunately, since cameras are not as clever as the human eye, they sometimes have trouble distinguishing between different types of light. This is because different light sources have what is known as different "color temperatures". This means that the color reflected from an object is different depending on the type of source light. For instance, the color reflected from a piece of white paper in direct sunlight will be different from that reflected from a piece of white paper under fluorescent lighting. Since the human eye is so sophisticated, it can compensate for these changes so that the original object always looks the same – the piece of paper always looks white. However, cameras cannot do this so they have to compensate with a function known as white balance to try and ensure that objects always appear the correct color, regardless of the light source.

When reviewing the white balance in an image on a camera's LCD panel it is not always possible to get an accurate impression of the effect due to the size of the screen. The only way to be completely sure is to view the image on a computer.

Digital cameras have a default setting for measuring the white balance in an image. This works by assessing the type of light in the image and then adjusting the white balance accordingly. However, this does not always work perfectly – particularly under artificial lighting – so manual adjustments can be made for different lighting conditions. These take into account different external and internal lighting conditions and usually cover: auto, shade, sunlight, cloudy, fluorescent, incandescent and flash. Adjusting the white balance settings is particularly useful in artificial lighting conditions and is worth experimenting with.

In most cases it is also possible to preset the white balance for certain shooting conditions. This involves selecting the appropriate white balance option from the camera's white balance menu. Once this has been done, place a piece of white or gray card at the point where you are going to capture the image. From the white balance menu select the option for manually recording the white balance and capture the image with the card in the center. The camera will then calculate the required white balance for these lighting conditions and adjust the lighting in the final image accordingly.

If you preset the white balance, make sure you set it to another mode (such as Auto) before you take a shot in different lighting conditions.

In the examples on the opposite page the top image was captured using an incorrect white balance setting (cloudy) resulting in an unnatural color cast in the image, while the one on the bottom used a correct setting (fluorescent). If in doubt about the lighting in a particular scene, capture it at several different white balance settings to ensure that at least one image will be correct.

I n the majority of photographic scenes there is one main light source. This can be used for exposure purposes and also to set the white balance as required. For instance, on a sunny day the white balance will be different from that of an indoor shot under fluorescent lighting.

However, in some instances you may be faced with a shot where there are different lighting sources. This is the case in the image below. The side lighting is provided by the sun coming through the window, while the room itself was lit by fluorescent lighting. The problem in cases like this is to judge the best white balance.

Take separate shots with different white balance settings

One way to deal with a scene like this is to take separate shots with different white balance settings, one for each type of light in the scene. This may work if one of the light sources is much stronger than the other. Another option is to leave the white balance setting on automatic and trust the camera to work it out. This is what was done in the image below and the auto white balance setting has correctly adjusted the image for the sunlight coming through the window from outside.

EXPOSURE AND METERING

Measuring the amount of light in a scene is crucial to the appearance of the final image. This section offers some tips about different methods for measuring light and how to apply these to create well-exposed images. It also explains the vital photographic technique of depth of field.

Covers

Understanding depth of field

Depth of field refers to the area within an image (from front to back) that is in focus. A large depth of field means that a large area of the image is in focus, while a small depth of field means that only a small area of the image is in focus. The depth of field for a particular image is determined by the focal length of the lens being used, the distance between the photographer, the main subject and the background, and, most importantly, the aperture being used.

The choice of depth of field to deploy will depend on the type of image you want to capture and this is where a bit of thought needs to go into the creative process: do you want an image with foreground, main subject and background in focus, or do you want to isolate the main subject with a blurred background? In general, landscape shots use a large depth of field (narrow aperture – large f-number) to keep everything in focus and single subject shots (such as portraits) benefit from a smaller depth of field (wide aperture – small f-number), thus causing the background to be blurred and giving more emphasis to the main subject.

Once you have mastered depth of field you will be able to start taking much more control over the technical side of your photography and also the composition of scenes.

The best way to take control over depth of field is to set your camera to aperture priority. This means that you can select the aperture and the camera will then automatically select a suitable shutter speed to expose the image correctly. Remember, a wide aperture will result in a faster shutter speed and vice versa. Also, the smaller the f-number, the wider the

> **The best way to take control over depth of field is to set your camera to aperture priority**

aperture, e.g. on some cameras f2.8 is the widest aperture while f22 is the narrowest. So to try and isolate a single image, select a wide aperture (f2.8, f4 or f5.6) and for a scene where you want as large an area as possible in focus, select a narrow aperture (f16 or f22). For an image where depth of field is not important select a mid-range aperture (f8 or f11) to give the best color saturation in the image. The image on the facing page was captured with an aperture of f16 to create a large depth of field to ensure that as much of the image was in focus as possible.

28 Softening the background

If the background in an image is too cluttered it may detract from the main subject.

One of the main uses for depth of field is to create a blurred background. The amount of blurring can be altered by changing the camera's aperture and this can be used to create differing effects. Each effect can produce a worthwhile image and it is up to you to decide the type of effect that you want to achieve for a particular photograph.

To create a blurred background, the camera has to be set on aperture priority mode so that you can manually select the aperture and the camera will then automatically set a suitable shutter speed. Start with a reasonably narrow aperture such as f11 (or the equivalent on a compact digital camera). This should render the background slightly blurry, as with the top image on the facing page. With a compact digital camera it may be hard to create a blurred depth of field because the internal architecture means that the lens is extremely generous in terms of depth of field: generally a much larger area will remain in focus than with a digital SLR camera. One way to try and create a narrow depth of field is to get as close in to the subject as possible and leave as large a distance as you can between the main subject and the background. Also, by using a zoom lens and zooming in on the main subject, a narrower depth of field will be created (i.e. less of the image will be in focus).

Aperture settings on compact digital cameras are equivalent to approximately 4 stops higher on a digital SLR camera. For instance, f2.8 on a compact is equivalent to f11 on a digital SLR. This is why it is hard to get good blurred effects with depth of field on a compact digital camera.

Once you have captured one image, widen the aperture on the camera: i.e. set it to a lower f-number. Take another image with an aperture of approximately f8 to see the difference between this image and the first one. The middle image on the facing page was captured with this setting, resulting in a greater degree of blurring in the background. For the final image, set the aperture to its widest setting, usually f4 or f5.6, and capture the image again. This will create an image with the greatest degree of blurring, as with the bottom image on the facing page. Depending on the image you require, you may want to use a greater or lesser amount of blurring.

USES

Some subjects that benefit from softening the background include children, flowers, insects and close-up objects that can be isolated with the background a reasonable distance behind.

Removing the background

In some instances you may want to use depth of field to completely blur the background. This is a technique that gives much greater emphasis to the main subject as there is no background to distract from the subject. It is an excellent option for close-up subjects and also portraits, as with the two images on the facing page.

When trying to remove the background by throwing it completely out of focus it is essential that you use the widest aperture setting on your camera. To do this you have to be in aperture priority (or manual) mode and set the aperture to its lowest f-number. This will be f2.8, f4, or f5.6, depending on the camera and type of lens. (Generally, the more expensive the lens, the wider you will be able to set the aperture.)

Some digital SLR cameras have a depth of field preview option that enables you to see the amount of an image that is going to be in focus at a particular aperture setting.

The next step is to position your background as far away as possible. If the background is too close it will enter the depth of field range of focus and so start showing unwanted detail.

Position your background as far away as possible

Then, get as close to the main subject as possible. Take some test shots to see how the background appears. If it is still too detailed, use the zoom function on your camera, even if it means moving slightly further away from the subject. As the lens is zoomed, the depth of field is reduced, i.e. less of the image is in focus. If you are using a zoom function, try using it at its maximum focal length to see how this affects the background.

Due to the forgiving nature of compact digital cameras (they are designed to try and ensure as much of an image as possible remains in focus) it may be difficult to completely blur the background of an image. If you want to use this technique then a digital SLR camera may be the answer.

SOFTWARE OPTION

Backgrounds can also be removed with image editing software by selecting the background and then adding various blur effects from the filters menu or the effects panel.

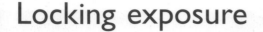

When measuring the amount of light in an image the main subject may not always be in the center of the image. This will usually be for composition purposes; invariably a better composition is achieved by not having the main subject in the middle of the frame. However, this can cause problems for the camera's metering system as it may not create the correct exposure for the main subject.

The way around this potential exposure problem is to use exposure lock. This is a technique whereby you take the exposure from one specific point, even though this is not the scene that you will finally capture. Once the meter reading has been taken, and the correct exposure has been set, the exposure can be locked for these settings. On some cameras this can

Take the exposure from one specific point, even though this is not the scene that you will finally capture

If your camera has an exposure lock button make sure this is kept held down while you recompose the scene. Otherwise the exposure setting will be lost.

be done with a dedicated Exposure Lock button on the camera. By pressing this the exposure is locked until the current shot is taken. This means that the scene can be recomposed by moving the camera and then the image captured. Since the exposure is still locked on the main subject this part of the image will be exposed correctly. Exposure lock can be used with any metering method within the camera.

If a camera does not have an Exposure Lock button the same effect can be achieved by pointing the camera at the area from which you want to take the exposure reading and half-depressing the shutter release button. This will take an exposure reading and also focus the camera with the auto-focus. Then, with the shutter release button still halfway depressed, the camera can be repositioned for the required scene.

In the top image on the facing page the dark sky has created an image where the boat does not stand out. In the bottom image the exposure was locked on the hull of the boat before the scene was recomposed and captured. Although the sky is over-exposed the boat is now exposed correctly.

Matrix metering

Measuring the amount of light in a scene is known as metering. Most cameras offer different options for the way this is done. In a lot of digital cameras the default metering option is the matrix method. This works by looking at areas within the whole scene and calculating the amount of light accordingly. This is done by comparing the image with a database compiled from thousands of images taken in a vast range of lighting conditions. The matrix method compares the current scene with those in the database and when it finds a similarly lit scene it applies the required shutter speed and aperture settings. The matrix method can be used successfully for the majority of photographic situations but it is not foolproof and can become confused by complex lighting conditions.

If light is spread evenly throughout an image then the matrix metering method should work well. However, if there are large dark and light areas within an image then this could cause problems for the matrix method and either sport metering or center-weighted metering should be used.

If you are unsure about light metering, leave the camera on matrix metering as this will work well in the majority of shooting situations.

In general, matrix metering can be used in most lighting conditions. The top image on the facing page looks as though it could cause problems for the matrix metering method, since the building is a lot lighter than the dark background. However, since there are reasonably equal areas of both light and dark in the image the matrix method can assimilate this and adjust the exposure accordingly. If either of the light or dark areas were significantly larger than the other then this could cause problems for the matrix method.

In general, matrix metering can be used in most lighting conditions

In the bottom image on the facing page the light and shade could potentially cause problems for the matrix method. However, since this is evenly distributed throughout the image the matrix method can easily find an equivalent image in its database and so expose the image correctly.

32 Spot metering

Spot metering is a method of measuring light in a scene that is less frequently used than matrix metering and one that is little understood by many camera users. However, although it is not such a common method it is still very important for specific types of lighting conditions.

Spot metering usually has to be specifically selected from within the camera's menu system (or sometimes from a dial on the camera body) and it works by taking a light reading from a very small area in the center of the viewfinder. The exposure for the scene is then set for this reading, regardless of the amount of light in the rest of the scene. For some scenes, this does not produce accurate results since the amount of light in the center of the scene may be different from that in other parts of the scene (matrix metering would be able to take this into account and expose the image correctly).

> **Spot metering works by taking a light reading from a very small area in the center of the viewfinder**

Spot metering is an excellent option for correctly exposing subjects against white or black backgrounds, as long as you are not worried about the exposure of the background.

The time to use spot metering is when it is important to expose one particular element of a scene correctly. This could be a very dark subject on a light background, or vice versa. However, the point where the spot metering reading is taken does not have to be in the center of the required scene. If necessary, a spot metering reading can be taken from anywhere in the scene and, using the exposure lock technique (see Tip 30), the scene can be recomposed and captured with the spot metering reading being retained.

In the top image on the facing page a spot meter reading was taken from the scene through the window, resulting in it being exposed correctly. However, since there was not enough light for the surrounding frame this is under-exposed, i.e. too dark. In order to get the frame exposed correctly, a spot metering reading was taken by pointing the camera at the frame, locking the exposure, and recomposing and capturing the scene. Although the frame is now correctly exposed the scene behind it is over-exposed, i.e. too light, since more light was needed to expose the frame.

More spot metering

As shown in the previous Tip, spot metering can be used to correctly expose certain areas within a scene. Depending on the area that is spot metered, this can result in the rest of the image being either over- or under-exposed. However, this does not mean that spot metering cannot be used to try and get the whole of a scene exposed correctly.

In photographic terms the darkest areas of an image are known as the shadows and the lightest areas are known as the highlights.

One situation where spot metering can be used is when there are large areas of dark and light within a scene: conditions could confuse a matrix meter reading. In cases like this a spot meter reading can be taken from a midtone area within the scene. A midtone is an area between the darkest and lightest areas within the image. If a spot metering is taken from here then there is more chance that the rest of the image will be correctly exposed too.

A midtone is an area between the darkest and lightest areas within the image

If a spot metering is being taken from an area that is off-center in the viewfinder then exposure lock will have to be used (unless the shot is being captured in fully manual mode, in which case the spot meter reading can be taken from the midtone area, and then the exposure settings can be applied before the scene is recomposed for shooting).

Spot metering can also be used to correctly expose single subjects against a particular background. In the top image on the facing page a matrix meter reading was taken initially, resulting in the main subject being under-exposed since the exposure was set for the larger area of water.

In the bottom image, a spot meter reading was taken from the fisherman before the image was recomposed for capturing the shot. The result is that the correct exposure has been achieved for the main subject since the meter reading was taken directly from this point. Since the fisherman is darker than the background, the water is now slightly over-exposed, but this serves to create a better contrast between the subject and the background, which results in a much more satisfactory image.

Exposure compensation

I n many digital cameras the internal light meter can become confused by certain situations, such as when there are very dark and very light areas within the same scene. Sometimes this can be adjusted by using a different method of metering from the default one. Another way of adjusting the exposure in a scene is to use exposure compensation.

Exposure compensation is regulated by the Exposure Value (EV) control on a camera. This is frequently a button on the body of the camera or sometimes it can be accessed from within the camera's menu. What the EV control does is allow more, or less, light into the camera for a particular exposure setting. This is usually measured in one step increments and each step up or down the scale is the equivalent of one exposure stop. For instance, if a +1 EV value is applied this is the same as reducing the shutter speed by one step or increasing the aperture by one step. The majority of digital camera can go to a minimum of +/−2 on the EV scale and some go as far as +/−5.

Some digital cameras deliberately under- or over-expose images. If you think this is the case, consider using +/−1 exposure compensation to see the difference this makes.

The reason that the EV control is important is because you can use it to physically change the amount of light entering the camera above or below the metering reading. In either aperture priority or shutter speed priority, the same amount of light will still enter the camera regardless of how you change one or other of the values. The EV control enables you to keep a particular aperture or shutter speed setting and then adjust the amount of light accordingly. This is useful if you need a certain aperture for depth of field or a shutter speed for freezing motion.

To make an image lighter, i.e. increase the exposure, use a positive EV value, and to make an image darker, i.e. decrease the exposure, use a negative EV value. In the top image on the facing page the aperture was set to f16 to achieve a reasonable depth of field in the image. However, the camera's metering system exposed the image for the pillars, leaving the background over-exposed. With the same aperture and shutter speed settings the EV value was set to −2 to try and decrease the exposure in the image, i.e. allow less light into the camera. The result is that the background is correctly exposed and although the pillars are now slightly under-exposed they have retained enough detail to create an effective overall image. If you experiment with the EV controls you will be able to capture well-exposed images in a variety of lighting conditions.

Center-weighted metering

Another metering mode is known as center-weighted metering. This is a method whereby the amount of light in the whole scene is measured but greater importance is given to the center of the frame. So if you are using this method of metering, your main subject should be in the center of the frame or you could use exposure lock while it is in the center and then recompose the scene.

Center-weighted metering is somewhere between matrix and spot metering and is particularly useful if you want to ensure that the main subject is properly exposed and as much of the background is properly exposed too. For this reason, it is a good option to try for portrait shots.

The top image below was taken with center-weighted metering, the middle one with matrix metering and the bottom one with spot metering.

36 Focus lock

Although it is a common photographic shot, it is not always desirable to have the main subject in the center of an image. It is natural to try and position a person or a famous landmark in the center of the viewfinder when capturing a shot. This can produce a pleasing image and it is always worth taking a few of these shots for every situation. However, it is also beneficial to experiment with some images where the main subject is not in the center. This can produce a more artistic and eye-catching composition (see Tip 80 for details about composing with the "rule of thirds" technique).

If you want to capture an image where the main subject is not in the center the crucial issue becomes focusing. By default, digital cameras focus on the element in the center of the viewfinder. If your subject is off-center then this could result in it being out of focus when the image is captured. (Some cameras have a function where you can select the area of focus from five or more pre-set areas within the viewfinder.)

The way to ensure that an off-center subject is in focus is to use focus lock. This works in the same way as exposure lock (discussed in Tip 30). To do this, focus on the subject in the center of the viewfinder by pressing the shutter release button halfway down. With the button still halfway depressed, recompose the scene and capture the image. The image below was captured in this way to create an interesting off-center composition.

If you take your finger off the shutter release button once focus lock has been activated, the focus will be lost and you will not be able to take the image until you re-focus.

37 Creating silhouettes

Silhouettes can be one of the most evocative and dramatic forms of photograph. They can be created from landscapes, buildings and people. In fact, almost any object can be turned into a silhouette in the correct lighting conditions.

The secret to creating a silhouette is in having a subject against a bright, backlit background. This will ensure that there is more light falling behind the subject than on the front of it. In a normal photograph this would probably produce a shaded subject that was still visible but not silhouetted. To turn the shaded subject into a silhouette it is usually necessary to take a metering reading from the backlit background. This will require locking the exposure on the background (see Tip 30 for details of how to do this). Once the exposure has been locked on the background, the shot can then be recomposed to include the foreground subject that will be rendered as the silhouette once the shot is taken. This happens because the exposure is set for the light background, i.e. there will be a reasonably fast shutter speed and a narrow aperture setting. This will allow enough light to enter the camera to expose the background correctly but there will not be enough for the foreground subject. This will result in the main subject being under-exposed, i.e. dark. Since the background is a lot lighter than the subject the under-exposure should be enough to create a black silhouette effect. If not, try locking the exposure on an even lighter area.

> **The secret to creating a silhouette is having a subject against a bright, backlit background**

Silhouettes of people can be captured using the technique described on this page. This adds an extra dimension to portraits and is a very effective option.

The image on the facing page was taken in the evening when the sun was setting. The exposure was locked on the orange glow in the sky, which provided a setting that was suitable to capture the sky and create the silhouette. The colors of the setting sun give an extra dimension to the silhouette and this is always worth bearing in mind when capturing this type of shot. Sometimes it is worthwhile taking another shot, with the exposure locked on a slightly darker area of the background, so that there is more definition visible in the main subject.

38

Dynamic range

The way the lightest and darkest areas within an image are depicted is known as the dynamic range of the image. Ideally, both extremes of the scale should still retain enough detail to be clearly identified. However, it is a known problem of most digital cameras that they are not ideal at always accurately capturing the full dynamic range in an image. This means that in some images the light areas will be too light (i.e. burned out) or the dark areas will be too dark.

To test the dynamic range of your own camera, find a location with one very dark and one very light area. Take two identical images, one with the exposure locked on the darkest area and one with the exposure locked on the lightest area (see Tip 30 for details about locking the exposure). This creates images like those below, neither of which is ideal.

One way around the problem of dynamic range is to take the same image at different exposure settings (bracketing – see Tip 11) and hope that one of them is acceptable. Another possible solution is to take a spot metering reading from a midtone area within the image and use this to capture the scene (see Tips 32 and 33 for details about spot metering). Luckily, dynamic range problems only occur in a small proportion of shooting conditions, but it is worth being aware of them so that you can make adjustments if required.

PEOPLE

People shots are frequently unsatisfactory as they can seem to be too easy to capture and so enough time is not taken with them. This section shows how to get the best out of people shots, in a variety of situations.

Covers

39

Distances and angles

For every image of people there are several variations that can be used to create markedly different results. This can be done by changing the distance from which the image is captured and also the angle.

The distance between the photographer and the subject can have a significant impact on the perception of anyone looking at the images. If an image is captured from a greater distance then the emphasis on the people will be reduced since the whole scene will have greater prominence. As you get closer to the subject for the shot the emphasis shifts from the background to the subject itself. Changing the shooting distance can be done by using the zoom on a digital camera or you can physically move closer. Of the two, using the zoom is probably better as you will not then be crowding the subject too much and they can relax more.

> The distance between the photographer and the subject can have a significant impact on the images

If you are too far away from the subject they will get lost in the background and the image will lose a lot of its impact and significance.

The top image on the facing page shows a subject taken from a distance, while the middle one is a medium range shot and the bottom one is a close-up. This results in the bottom image having a much greater impact. Which type you choose depends on what you want to convey. If you want to show people in context then shooting from further away is better.

As well as changing the shooting distance it can also be beneficial to change the angle of shooting. This can create a very different impression for the same subject. For instance, a shot from below can create an imposing impression while one from the side is more relaxed. Similarly a shot taken from above creates an image with a greater sense of space, as if the subject were looking up into the sky.

GETTING LOW

Sometimes it pays to lie down on the ground and capture an image from this angle as it creates a better perspective.

40 Group shots

Everyone likes looking at images of other people, whether they be family snapshots or group shots in the workplace. However, not everyone enjoys having their picture taken and this can cause problems for the photographer. The issue is exacerbated when groups of people are involved: not only do you have to try and ensure that everyone is looking enthusiastic about posing for a photo but you also have to try and compose and capture the image so that everyone is positioned correctly and looking in the right direction.

One of the crucial issues when creating group photographs is timing. Initially it is important to give people enough time before you plan to capture the image. People usually like to prepare

Always take several group shots since there will invariably be someone blinking or looking the wrong way.

Give people enough time before you plan to capture the image

themselves before having their photo taken so let them know what you are planning to do. It is also important to give yourself enough time, both before you take the shot and while you are doing it. The more time you have for composing and capturing the shot, the more time there will be to get everyone relaxed and enjoying the experience.

As far as the composition of group shots is concerned, it is not ideal to have a straight line of people (see top image on the facing page). This is not only clichéd, it can also look very stiff and awkward. As a simple variation, get people in the group to stand side-on to you and then turn their heads to face the camera. This is a more relaxed pose and will instantly give the image a more natural appearance. Also, try arranging people in different locations, such as in the bottom image on the facing page.

Another option for a group composition is to organize the subjects in different positions: standing, sitting, kneeling and even lying down. (If you plan this beforehand you can save time when it comes to shooting.) Props are also a good way of adding interest: give people something to hold or arrange them around nearby objects. Group shots need not be either staid or conventional: the more inventive you are, the more the subjects will enjoy the experience and respond well.

Capturing activities

Although portrait shots of adults and children are great for framing and putting on the wall, more interesting images can be captured of people when they are involved in some form of activity. This could be something physical, such as playing sport, or something more contemplative, such as reading. Whatever the activity, this type of shot has the benefit that the subject is not usually posing and so it provides a more natural result than a formally posed image.

The first thing to do when capturing an activity shot is to select the activity and the appropriate surroundings. (Although in some cases it may just be a question of seeing a suitable shot, such as your child reading a book, and taking it immediately.) If possible, try and capture activities in their natural environment as this gives a general context to the activity.

When capturing activities make sure you have the correct camera settings already applied. This will save you from having to fiddle around with the camera when you could be capturing action shots.

An important element of activity shots is the use of a zoom lens (use the optical zoom on your camera if it has one, rather than the digital zoom). This is because you should be a reasonable distance away from your subject so that you do not crowd them (as with the images on the facing page). If possible, the subject should be unaware that you are there. To try and achieve this, find a suitable shooting position and stay there for a period of time so that you are not so noticeable to your subject.

You should be a reasonable distance away from your subject so that you do not crowd them

When it comes to capturing a particular activity the camera settings will depend on the type of shot you are taking. For someone reading a book you may want to use a wide aperture (low f-number) to try and blur the background so that they stand out more. For a sporting activity, you may want to use a fast shutter speed to try and freeze the action. However, with any type of activity shot that involves movement there may be a bit of trial and error involved. But if you work out beforehand what you are trying to achieve you will be better placed to capture the image when the moment arrives.

PEOPLE

42 Candid shots

A good portrait may adorn your wall or mantelpiece for many years and it is one of the most common ways to capture images of people. But un-posed, or candid, shots can be just as appealing and they offer a different type of insight into the character of the subject.

The best way to capture candid shots is to ensure that the subject is unaware of your presence with a camera. If there are other people around you can try blending in with them, or place yourself behind an object such as a car or a pillar (but make sure it does not look as though you are spying on the subject). Another, perhaps better, option is to use a camera with a powerful zoom function. This will enable you to stand far enough away from the subject so that they do not think you are trying to photograph them.

The best way to capture candid shots is to ensure that the subject is unaware of your presence

Make sure you don't intrude on people's privacy by capturing images of anyone who would prefer not to be photographed. In the case of children, make sure their parents don't object.

Patience is the key when capturing candid shots: sometimes you will have to wait several minutes until you get the right image (since you cannot tell the subject what you want them to do). In some ways it is similar to capturing images of wildlife, in that you have to make yourself inconspicuous and then be prepared to wait.

The top image on the facing page was taken with a zoom lens of 300mm. It is unusual in that it is not a typical "children" image – the lack of motion emphasizes the idea of waiting. Try and capture people while they are doing something out of the ordinary. This will make for a more interesting image as it shows them out of their normal context.

Candid shots do not have to be static and the bottom image on the facing page conveys a sense of action and also a certain trepidation. The reaction of the children is what makes the image interesting and conveys the emotion of the moment. The motion also ensures that their attention is completely diverted from the camera, thereby creating the unguarded pose.

Posed options

One option for people shots is when individuals are deliberately posing for you, preferably with an interesting costume or act. In many tourist centers around the world, or at festivals, there are street performers who make excellent subjects for photographers. They are usually flamboyant characters with colorful costumes and props, so there is a lot of scope for experimentation. As with all people shots, take your time to get the best vantage point (this may involve waiting until the initial crowds have subsided) and try to get the subject in as interesting a pose as possible. Also, make sure you put some money in their hat or collecting bucket, if there is one, as then they may be more likely to create a specific pose for you.

Filling the frame

One technique for capturing portraits is to fill the frame with as much of the subject's face as possible. This can create a very powerful effect since every feature of the face is detailed in the image. This type of image is frequently used for politicians and business people as it conveys a sense of control and it can also look slightly intimidating. Look at some newspapers and magazines to see how these types of images are used to illustrate certain types of story.

When capturing this type of image it is vital to use a zoom lens and the bigger the better. To create the same effect without a zoom would result in you being only inches away from the subject's face, which is unlikely to result in a natural-looking image.

Initially, try zooming in so that there is still a slight border around the subject's face. Then, take another shot where their whole face fills the viewfinder or the LCD panel. Finally, try and take a shot so that only their main features are visible. Compare the three shots to see the different visual effects that they create.

Take another shot where their whole face fills the viewfinder or the LCD panel

If you want to add extra emphasis to this type of shot this can be achieved by capturing the subject from below their eye line. If you shoot up towards someone and fill the frame the resultant image will look as if they are towering over you, with all of their features clearly depicted.

Another option for this type of image is to convert it to black and white once it has been captured. The top image on the facing page conveys the sense of detail and expression in the features, while the bottom image has an extra dimension in black and white.

BLACK AND WHITE

Images can be converted to black and white in image editing software by removing the color from an image. Some cameras can also capture black and white images.

45 Children

There are probably more digital images captured of children than any other subject. Digital cameras are ideal for this purpose as you can take an almost limitless number of pictures and children can then immediately look at them to see the results. Children who grow up with digital cameras expect to be able to see the pictures on the camera's LCD panel and if they are ever faced with a film camera they may be perplexed because they cannot see the final images.

One of the main problems when capturing images of children is that they tend to perform a passable impression of perpetual motion. They are rarely still for very long so it can be a challenge to try and capture effective images of them. Another factor that can make this worse is the time lag that is inherent with most compact digital cameras. Frequently when capturing images of children, you will take what you think is a perfect shot but the time lag will result in an image in which the child has blinked just at the moment when the actual shot was taken. One way to try and overcome this is to use the continuous shooting mode, if your camera has one (see Tip 74 for details), or work out the time lag and try and factor this into the photographic equation.

Children tend to perform a passable impression of perpetual motion

Let children practice with digital cameras as this helps them learn about photography and it also makes them more comfortable around cameras when it comes to capturing images of them.

Portraits of children are familiar photographic subjects and there is absolutely nothing wrong with a standard, face-on portrait. However, in addition to this, try to capture portraits that offer something slightly different: put the children in an unusual or picturesque location or include additional elements in the image such as flowers or family pets. In the top image on the facing page the composition of the child and the rope ladder gives the portrait a different perspective and a more relaxed aspect.

Capturing images of children involved in an activity is an excellent option too. This is because their attention is diverted and there is also the activity itself to help make the image more interesting. In the bottom image on the facing page the activity of feeding pigeons gives the image a sense of motion and the child is concentrating on the activity rather than the camera.

46 Relaxed portraits

When capturing portraits of either adults or children the biggest problem is the obvious presence of the camera, particularly if it is a posed, formal portrait. One partial solution is to use a zoom lens so that you are further away from the subject and they do not feel too pressurized by the camera. Also, try putting the camera on a tripod and use a remote control (if you have one) to activate the shutter release. This means that you can detach yourself from the camera and talk to the subject in a relaxed fashion. Be aware of your surroundings too and try and make them as inviting as possible: make sure the room is uncluttered and that the subject is comfortable.

Another factor when capturing portraits is to make the subject as relaxed as possible. Talk to them before you start taking pictures and tell them what you want to do. In some cases it will be beneficial to give the subject some type of prop (especially if children are involved). To try and capture the best facial expression, ask the subject to look down and close their eyes. Then, on the count of three, ask them to open their eyes and look up. If you capture the image at this point it should create a more natural expression as the subject will be less self-conscious.

47 Family gatherings

Families can be stressful at the best of times but when it comes to capturing photographs of family gatherings it can be a near-impossible task. For events such as weddings and family parties, determination and perseverance are required.

At an event such as a wedding one of the quickest and easiest ways of capturing large group shots is just to copy the official photographer (if there is one). They will create all of the poses and you can then stand beside or behind them and capture the same images (try and stand just behind since if you are at the side the group will be looking at the photographer rather than you). If you do not have an official photographer to act as a guide you will have to take control yourself and be reasonably forceful with everyone. Decide beforehand the types of shots that you want to capture and take as many shots as you can to take into account people blinking and looking the other way when the shot is being taken. Try creating themed shots, i.e. images of all one generation or notable groupings of family members.

ARCHITECTURE

Architecture offers great photographic opportunities in terms of structures, patterns and details. This section contains tips for capturing all aspects of buildings and architecture and also shows how to constructively combine other elements into these types of shots.

Covers

Finding the right spot

When capturing images of buildings and architecture there are a number of "standard" views. For instance, a straight-on shot of the Eiffel Tower or the Taj Mahal. These are instantly recognizable iconic images and it is always worth capturing a few of these if you are in this type of location. However, what you will end up with is essentially a picture postcard image. This is useful and effective for some purposes such as showing friends and relations but it is also advisable to try and capture some more creative shots to show a more individual side of a building.

Never put yourself in physical danger when trying to find the right spot for capturing images. Sometimes it is better to ignore a shot than to risk injury.

When you are faced with a shot of a building or architecture the first thing to do is to take some of the conventional shots, just to make sure that you have got these taken care of. Even when you do this, try and avoid the crowds by capturing your images either early in the morning or later in the afternoon or evening.

Once you have captured the traditional shots you can then concentrate on finding a location from where you can capture more individual and artistic shots. The first thing to do is to walk around the building and look at it from every angle (depending on the building this may take some time but it is worth persevering with). Then you will be able to assess potential shots that show the building in a different context from the standard view. Look for close-ups to

Concentrate on finding a location from where you can capture more individual and artistic shots

show the building's character, use the building's angles to show symmetry and patterns and change your own angle to alter the perspective (try getting above the building and also lying down and shooting from directly below part of the building).

The top image on the facing page is a "standard" one of the La Pedrera building in Barcelona, as it appears on many postcards. The bottom image is the same building but shot from much closer and directly from the pavement below, thereby highlighting the character of the building more.

Capturing the best light

As shown in Tip 23 the Golden Hour is the time just after sunrise and just before sunset when the light has a rich, golden color which is perfect for photography (presuming the sun is out and there is not heavy cloud cover). Sometimes as a photographer you stumble across this type of light, but more often than not you have to make the effort to be in the right place at the right time to capture images with this type of light.

The first thing to do when trying to capture the best light is to check the times of sunrise and sunset. You can then decide on the location from where you want to capture images and work out when you need to be there in relation to the sunrise and sunset times. Make sure you are at your location at least half an hour (preferably one hour) before the ideal time you have calculated for photography. This is to allow yourself time to get set up and select potential shots and also to take some shots in the current lighting conditions so that you can compare these to the Golden Hour ones.

Even if you think you have missed the best light it can still pay dividends to wait a few minutes to make sure that the sun is not going to reappear or there are not some other shots that can be captured.

Make sure you are at your location at least half an hour before the ideal time you have calculated for photography

After checking the sunrise and sunset times you should then check the overall weather forecast: there may be little point in trying to capture the early morning or evening sun if it is going to be heavily overcast. The best sort of conditions are generally clear skies with some broken cloud. This should still allow the Golden Hour sun to illuminate your subjects and the cloud will provide additional color for sunsets and silhouettes.

Sometimes, even with diligent planning, you will come across the best light quite by chance. Both of the images on the facing page and the following two pages were captured about 20 minutes after it seemed the sun had gone down and disappeared. However, I waited another half an hour and the sun reappeared, allowing for these images with the rich, golden light.

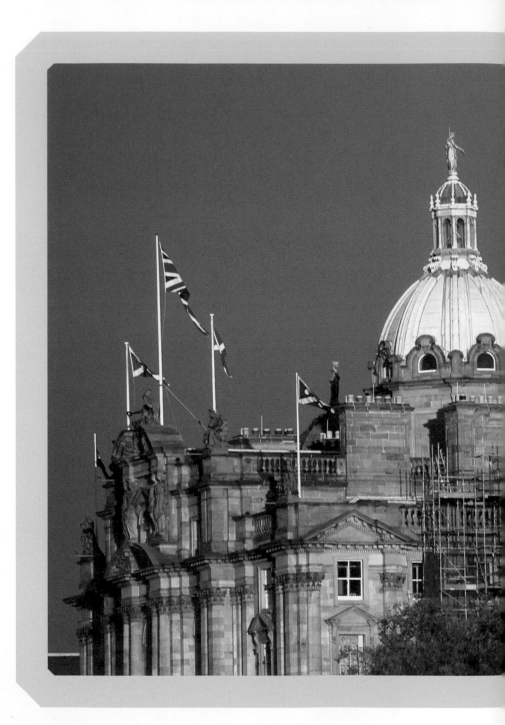

50   Using the angles

A lot of shots of buildings are taken as straight-on, two-dimensional images. While this can create highly effective photographs, it would be wrong to concentrate on this type of image exclusively. Buildings are frequently a fascinating combination of curves and angles that can create a much broader context for them.

Vanishing points are a good option when working with angles. This is where two lines meet in the distance. Straight roads and bridges can be used to create effective vanishing point images, particularly if they are positioned in the center of the frame or scene.

All buildings have angles and these are a rich source of photographic opportunities. Angles can be used to emphasize the size of a building. The image on the facing page is an example of this. The size of the tower is emphasized by the angles of the structure and this gives it a completely different character from that seen in a straight-on shot from further away. For this it is essential to find the right spot from which to capture the angles of the building or structure.

The image on this page was created using the angles of the building by capturing it at 45 degrees from the corner. This gives a sense of perspective and the patterned effect that is achieved creates a more interesting image than a standard straight-on one.

51 Emphasizing size

Showing the size of a building or piece of architecture is an excellent way to display its context. Different techniques can be used to show the imposing nature of a building, or represent it as a small part of its surrounding area. Either way, it is a useful option for revealing some of the character of a building.

As shown in the previous Tip the size of a building can be emphasized by capturing an image from directly below it. This creates a sense of perspective and can be used to exaggerate the size of a structure.

Another option for emphasizing the size of a building is to make it look relatively small compared to its surroundings, even if it is a large structure. The best way to do this is to use a wide angle lens to capture as much of the surrounding area as possible. If there are other objects in the picture that can be used to contrast with the size of the building then so much the better. In the image below the stature of the cranes serves to show the comparatively diminutive size of the structure below, while they create an eye-catching composition in their own right.

52 Keep your distance

Famous landmarks are a justifiable source of great photographic opportunities. Any photographer can capture a world-famous landmark and, in general, it is fairly easy to capture this type of shot. Around the world the majority of landmarks are made very accessible: tour buses and tour parties visit them on a regular basis and you need never feel short of company when you are capturing images. However, when you are taking pictures of landmarks you should always walk around the building and try to get a different vantage point (as shown in Tip 48 at the start of this section).

Another option when capturing images of landmarks is to try and put some distance between yourself and the crowds of other sightseers (tour parties usually choose the closest point to a landmark site). Walk away from the landmark and try and find a vantage point that takes in the whole of the building. If you can include other parts of the location too then this will help place it in context.

Try and capture images of well-known landmarks with no one else visible in the shot. This will focus attention on the main subject rather than any other people.

The image on this page was taken by walking through a local park before capturing this shot of the Sagrada Familia cathedral in Barcelona. This not only hides the other tourists; it also enables the foreground pond to be included in the image.

Concentrating on detail

By their very nature most buildings are made out of numerous small elements that are combined to create the whole structure. However, frequently when we capture images we concentrate on the overall building rather than its constituent parts. This can be a great oversight as there is a wealth of photographic material in the detail of buildings.

Details help to convey the character of buildings, rather than their overall appearance. This can cover a multitude of elements: windows, door handles, artwork, tiles and stone structures. In fact, almost anything that is part of a building.

A useful way to capture detail in a building is to start from a distance from where you can capture the whole building and then work your way closer and closer to capture the details. This can be used as a series of images to show different aspects of the same structure, and each of the images should be able to stand up in its own right as well.

The image below is a long-distance shot of a building with a number of modern design features. The top image on the facing page shows the details of one particular side of the building. The bottom image on the facing page is a close-up of a single window within the wall above. This reveals some of the design features of the building and provides an interesting contrast to the long-distance image.

Building details are excellent for conveying textures and design features.

Using patterns

Patterns are all around us: natural patterns, artificial patterns, symmetrical patterns and asymmetrical patterns. Whenever you have a camera with you it is always a good habit to look for images that contain patterns.

When capturing patterns it is usually best to use a zoom lens so that the pattern can fill as much of the frame as possible. This gives the pattern added impact as there are no other elements in the image to detract from it.

Patterns can be used to highlight a certain feature or characteristic of a subject or they can be used in their own right just as an artistic image. The image below displays an irregular pattern of scaffolding that conveys the industrial nature of the structure. By using a zoom lens the complexity of the structure is displayed by showing the way in which the elements in the pattern interact.

The top image on the facing page is a pattern that stands on its own and it is given an extra dimension through the use of color in the window boxes. The bottom image on the facing page is a symmetrical pattern that serves to convey the ornate character of the building. By concentrating on this type of pattern the image helps to demonstrate the ordered and artistic nature of the structure. Sometimes, close-up patterns can reveal more about a building than a wide-angle shot.

55 Combining elements

A common technique for architecture shots is to include foreground objects to create a perspective and context for the shot. Another option is to include the foreground object as an integral part of the shot, by effectively combining it with the main subject.

To create the most effective combination of two elements it is best for the foreground object to be at least as large as the background one, if not larger. Trees and bushes are excellent for this, as shown in the image on the facing page. Try and organize the composition of the image so that there is enough of the background object visible, but not too much so that it dominates the whole shot. Think of the foreground and the background as being on separate layers and organize these so that they are combined to make the final image.

A similar, if slightly more artistic, effect can be created with image editing software when separate images are physically combined. This is done by using the Layers function where one image is placed on top of another and then the software is used to determine how much of the bottom image shows through the top one. There are numerous options for how this is done and it is a highly effective way of creating an edited combination image, as shown below.

To combine elements with image editing software, capture two specific images with this in mind. For instance, one image of a building and another of a texture, such as a plant or water.

Including foreground elements

Architecture shots can be both dramatic and artistic. Sometimes an image of a building itself is enough to create a compelling photograph. The size and character of a building can frequently be captured in an image without any additional elements and this is always a good option for buildings.

Even though images of buildings on their own can be effective there are times when it is a good idea to include other objects in the foreground of the image. This can serve to give context to the image (for instance, a national flag in an image can create a geographical context) or just to brighten up what would be a good, but not stunning, image.

Foreground objects do not have to dominate the image and sometimes "less is more" is a good maxim for this type of shot. In the top image on the facing page the flowers in the foreground only take up a small proportion of the picture but the eye is immediately drawn to them because of the vibrant colors. This

Sometimes "less is more" is a good maxim for this type of shot

leads you into the image and after the foreground object has been noticed the eye is then drawn to the main subject. Without the flowers, the image would have been an unexceptional one.

The bottom image on the facing page has a greater emphasis on the foreground objects, in this case the trees. This shot was taken as one of a series of images, of which some included foreground objects and some did not. The inclusion of the foreground trees gives a better sense of the building's location and provides a contrast to the modern architecture.

OPTIONS

Some of the types of objects that can be included in the foreground of an architecture shot include trees, plants, statues, street lamps, vehicles and even people. Take time to compose the objects in relation to the building.

57 Dealing with distortion

One problem with lenses in digital cameras is that the glass is slightly curved. In certain conditions this can result in elements within an image looking distorted. This tends to be particularly obvious in images of buildings. The problems

can also be made worse if a zoom lens is used. In the image on the left, the church spire appears at an angle, although this is an optical effect caused by the camera lens. Since the spire is at the side of the image (where the lens is most curved) the distortion has been made worse. Always check images of buildings to see if they look distorted or at an angle. If this is the case then there are some steps that can be taken to try and reduce the distortion (see below for details).

58 Avoiding distortion

If your images of buildings suffer from distortion there are a few options for trying to rectify this. One is to position the main subject in the center of the frame rather than at one of the sides. Another step is to move further away from the subject: the closer you are, the more pronounced the distortion. If you are further away from the subject then the curve of the lens will be more forgiving. Similarly, if there is already distortion in an image, the use of zoom will exaggerate this even further.

Another option for removing distortion is to use a dedicated architecture lens. This is a specialist lens that is designed to eliminate the curvature of the lens. However, these types of lenses tend to be expensive and generally can only be used on digital SLR cameras. However, if you are taking a lot of architecture photography these types of lenses may be worth looking at.

LANDSCAPES

Landscape photographs can create some stunning images if done properly. This section shows how to take control over landscape photography and make the scenes work for you. This includes creating specific moods, adding objects of interest, combining different elements, using color effectively and even adding your own props.

59 Create your scene

In some cases, stunning landscape images will come to you: a beautiful sunrise or sunset, or a desert landscape highlighted by a single, lone tree. However, on other occasions you will have to put a bit more effort into your shots and actively go out and create a scene with the elements at your disposal.

One way to create effective scenes is to combine existing elements, such as natural landscapes and constructed objects. If you are doing this, try and locate the constructed element first and then work this into the composition. The image below was created in this way. The line of benches had to be captured at a specific angle to ensure that they formed a line to draw the viewer's eye through the image. Without the benches the image would have been unremarkable. Think of yourself as an artistic chef trying to mix all of the right ingredients together to get the best end result.

It may be permissible to move objects within a scene, or add them to a scene if necessary. However, make sure you are not interfering with anything else and always replace any objects that you use in your scene.

Flattening the perspective

Combining the background of a scene with a foreground object is a common way of creating added interest (see Tip 55 for more details). This can be used to show the surroundings of the main subject or to produce an interesting perspective by making the foreground object look proportionally larger than the background.

Another way of combining foreground and background objects is to flatten the perspective between them to make the foreground object seem closer to the background than it really is. To do this you require a background that is relatively free of other objects, so that they do not interfere with the perspective effect by providing something else by which to judge the position of the foreground object. Once you have selected your foreground object and background you have to combine the two by using the greatest focal length on your camera's lens: i.e. zoom in on the foreground object as much as possible. This will create the appearance of the background becoming closer than it really is. In the image below, of the Grand Canyon, the distance between the tree and the background is nearly one mile, but through the use of a zoom lens and an uncluttered scene it looks a lot less.

LANDSCAPES

117

Re-orientating a landscape

As shown in Tip 9 an image can be dramatically changed by altering the orientation of the camera. This can be done to capture different parts of a similar scene and it can also be used to give a completely different character to shots of exactly the same scene.

The orientation of a particular scene will depend on the effect and impact that you want to create. In simple terms, a landscape image concentrates on the horizontal nature of a scene, while a portrait image concentrates on the vertical elements. Even within the same scene this can produce differing visual effects.

A landscape image can be used to emphasize the physical width of a scene, such as a sprawling mountain range or a sweeping row of houses. By contrast, a portrait image can be used to emphasize the area surrounding the subject of an image, such as the land, sea or sky. Both produce very distinctive, but different, results.

By simply re-orientating the image from landscape to portrait it becomes much more effective

In the top image on the facing page the landscape orientation highlights the band of houses in the middle of the scene. It is a reasonable image, but nothing dramatic. However, by simply re-orientating the image from landscape to portrait it becomes much more effective. The band of houses is now dwarfed by both the sea and the sky and they take a much greater prominence in the image than in the landscape version. This serves to concentrate on the isolation of the houses by showing that they are faced with imposing elements both above and below them. It is always worth changing the orientation of a landscape image if only to try and change the emphasis of the scene.

ALWAYS RE-ORIENTATE

For any landscape it is always worth taking shots in landscape and portrait mode. You are not wasting film and you may never visit the scene again.

62 Creating moods

Luckily it is not essential to use the Golden Hour (see Tip 23) to capture images in good photographic lighting conditions. All types of lighting can be used to capture images and the only constraint is your own imagination. When different lighting conditions are available they can be used to create different types of mood within an image.

Low-level or dull lighting is often thought of as being un-conducive to good photographs. However, this can be an excellent opportunity to capture atmospheric images. This type of light usually has an even quality, so different exposure levels throughout the image become less of an issue. Frequently on cloudy days an hour

Low-level lighting can be an excellent opportunity to capture atmospheric images

or so before sunset this type of light can be used to produce very natural-looking images. The top image on the facing page was captured in the late evening on a cloudy day and it helps to create a mood of tranquility and serenity. Due to the lighting levels a tripod was used to keep the camera steady, since a shutter speed of 1/15th second was needed to maintain a narrow aperture for a large depth of field – to keep as much of the image in focus as possible.

A change in the weather is another opportunity for creating mood images. For instance, the dark clouds of an incoming storm make a dramatic backdrop to landscape images and can be used to emphasize the power of nature in an image. An approaching rain storm is ideal for conveying the mood of changing weather.

Sunsets and sunrises are also valuable for conveying the mood of change, in this case the change in the day. The bottom image on the facing page creates a mood for the end of the day, which is emphasized by there still being some detail in the foreground. For this type of image, take an exposure reading from a midtone (or darker) area of the sky to ensure that the foreground does not become under-exposed and hence rendered as a silhouette (see Tip 37 to see how to create silhouettes).

If you are capturing images of storms this can be most effective just before the storm breaks. Try and get indoors before the storm itself arrives.

63 Including objects of interest

The human eye is naturally drawn to objects or items that stand out in an image. For instance, a contrasting color or an unusual object will catch the eye, especially within landscape scenes. When dealing with landscapes it is always a good idea to try and look for objects of interest and include them in the scene in some way.

Objects of interest can include almost anything depending on the scene. For instance, a red flower in a field of white ones will catch the attention, as will an incongruous object in a landscape scene, such as a lone house amongst a range of hills.

Aim to try and create a "road map" that can guide the viewer through the image

When using objects of interest within a scene the aim is to try and create a "road map" that can guide the viewer through the image. Ideally, they should notice the object of interest first and then be able to follow their way through the rest of the image from there.

Sometimes it pays to wait for objects of interest to appear in your scene. For instance, if you know a train is due at a particular time it could enhance your shot to wait for this and include it in the scene.

In the top image on the facing page, the bridge structure acts as the initial object of interest. The eye is then drawn to the landscape behind the bridge and this creates an image that would have been fairly standard without the bridge in it. This type of image can frequently be captured in the country and so it is always good to get into the habit of searching for buildings or structures when you are in this type of location.

The bottom image on the facing page contains a much smaller object of interest, the fisherman in red at the side of the image. Although this is a small part of the image it is enhanced by the reflection and creates an interesting road map. The eye is initially drawn across the front of the image to the person in red. It then travels up the river bank to the point where the river and the trees meet. Even though the object of interest is small in this scene it still catches the attention because of the color contrast with the background and the rest of the image.

64 Story telling

As shown in Tip 27, depth of field can be used to present more, or less, of an image in focus. As well as being a technical photographic operation this can also be used as a composition feature.

The way depth of field can be incorporated into the composition of an image is to use a large depth of field (i.e. a lot of the image area in focus) to tell a story within the scene. This is not a story in the sense of a narrative but, like a story, it has a beginning, a middle and an end. In photographic terms, depth of field can be used to create the equivalent in a scene. For instance, in the image below the boat is the beginning as it is at the front of the image, the sea and land behind the boat are the middle and the sky behind is the end. By including these elements in an image you can show the location, context and characteristics of the scene.

All stories do not follow exactly the same formula. The same is true for story-telling images and they do not have to follow such a linear structure as the one below. The image on the facing page has the same story-telling elements: the tree is the beginning, the scenery the middle and the sky the end. However, the tree takes on much more prominence since it covers both the middle and the end elements. This does not mean it is a better or worse story-telling image, just a different one. The same elements could also be composed in a similar way to those in the image on this page.

Look at all of the elements in a scene to see how each one can be best used to improve the overall composition of the image.

For story-telling images, set the camera to aperture priority mode and select an aperture of f16 or f22 to ensure that as much of the image as possible is in focus.

65 Adding props

Landscape scenes are sometimes enough on their own for the photographer. Mountain ranges or desert scenes are excellent photographic opportunities that generally do not require too much additional assistance. On some occasions, it is beneficial to include other elements such as naturally occurring foreground objects in the scene. However, there are other times when the scene in front of you requires a little more assistance and this is where adding props comes in.

Props are any additional element that you specifically add into an image. This can be done for several reasons. Firstly, you may want to add objects to create a context for the scene. For instance, a mountain scene may benefit from a pair of strategically placed walking boots in the foreground. Similarly, a desert scene would be given additional impact with a near-empty bottle of water in the foreground.

> ## You may want to add objects to create a context for the scene

Another reason for adding props is to provide some contrasting color and act as a focal point in the image. In the top image on the facing page the red tube draws the initial attention and the eye is then drawn further up to the mountain.

Props can also be used to provide a contrast to a scene. For instance, a very modern prop could be inserted into an old-fashioned scene, or a small prop could be used to emphasize the size of a building.

Don't take any props with you that are too bulky or heavy. This may inhibit your chances of getting to particular locations. There is no point having a prop with you if you cannot get to the place to use it.

HUMOR

Props can add a humorous touch to an image but make sure that you do not use anything offensive to people.

When dealing with props you can rely on objects that you find when you are out on location (as in the bottom image on the facing page) or you can actively take props with you when you are going to shoot a particular subject. This takes a little bit of planning and organization but it can pay dividends in creating images with humorous or interesting effects.

66

Bands of color

Color is all around us and the human eye can differentiate millions of different colors and shades. In photographic terms, color is an essential ingredient, but it is not always necessary to include as many colors as possible for effective images. It is always good practice to think about color in images and the best way in which it can be used.

One way to use color in images is to show an extravagant or vibrant event such as a festival or a carnival. Colorful costumes and designs can then be used to capture a flavor of the event and it is an excellent way to get some very striking images.

Another, perhaps more understated, way of using color is to look for large blocks of color in a scene and see if they can be incorporated into a meaningful image. Bands of color can be used either horizontally or vertically; three good options are the sky, the sea and grassed areas such as fields and parks.

The use of bands of color can be made to highlight other items in the image by creating a "sandwich" effect. This is where the bands of color are above and below the main subject. This displays the center area as the filling in the sandwich, while the colored areas are still noteworthy in their own right. This is the case in the top image on the facing page, where the blue sky and green park act as the two areas of color that are highlighting the band in the center of the image.

> Bands of color can be made to highlight other items in the image by creating a "sandwich" effect

Bands of color are just as effective if they are used vertically, as in the bottom image on the facing page, where the green of one side of the field contrasts with the yellow–golden appearance of the other half. With this type of scene it is important to locate yourself in the right position, so that the line between the two bands of color is in the middle. This will split the colored bands and also draw the viewer's eye through the middle of the image to the back.

67

Reflections

One of the great qualities of water is that it creates reflections and these can be incorporated into photographs in a variety of ways. The most obvious way is in the reflection of landscapes or objects such as buildings or bridges that are located near water.

The classic reflection shot is one where the water is very still so that the object and its reflection look as similar as possible, as in the image on the facing page. Lakes are the best for this type of shot. Ideally, try visiting them on a day when there is very little wind. With faster-moving water, such as streams and rivers, it is still perfectly possible to get good reflection shots. This creates a rippled effect in the reflection and, as long as it is not too extreme, this can result in a very pleasing image.

Another option for reflection shots is to take a more proactive role and deliberately create artistic effects. One way to do this is to throw a stone into a pool or lake and then capture the shot including the resulting ripples, as shown in the image below.

68 Panoramas

Digital cameras have proved to be very successful and popular at creating panoramas. These are two or more images of a scene that is too large to be captured in a single shot. The successive images are stitched together to give one panoramic image. Panoramas can be created in image editing software programs and a lot of digital cameras also have a facility for creating them within the camera.

When capturing images for a stitched panoramic scene make sure that you capture the different images from the same location and at the same exposure settings. If possible, use a tripod to ensure the same point of shooting and overlap each image by approximately 20% so that the stitching appears seamless.

Another way to create panoramas is to capture an image and then crop it so that it appears in a panoramic format. In order to do this, capture the image at the camera's highest possible resolution. This will enable you to crop the image and still print it out at a large size (see Tip 10 for details on cropping and image size.) The panorama across these two pages was created in this way, with the source image being the top one on the facing page. This serves to isolate one part of the image and create a panoramic effect because of its dimensions.

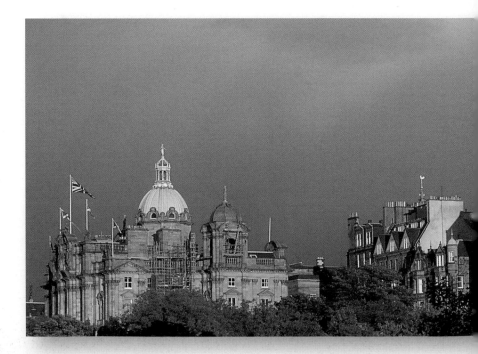

Green compensation

A lot of shooting situations have their own quirks and curiosities and one unusual thing about landscape photography is that there is often a lot of the color green in the scene. In a lot of cases, a camera's internal light meter gets confused if there is a lot of green and as a result it does not select the correct exposure. In this situation, you should deliberately take an exposure reading from the area of green within the image (see Tip 30 for details on how to lock the exposure in an image).

If the exposure is taken from the green area in a scene then the rest of it should be evenly exposed. However, one quirk about this is that the result tends to be under-exposed by approximately 2/3 stops. To compensate for this, use exposure compensation (see Tip 34 for details) to ensure the correct exposure. Set the EV control to −2/3 and then recapture the image. The image on the left was captured after taking a meter reading from the green foliage, without using exposure compensation. The image on the right was taken with the same exposure and an exposure compensation of −2 to get the correct exposure.

MOTION

Even though digital photography is a static medium there are still numerous ways in which it can be used to convey the impression of motion. This section contains tips for different ways in which motion can be depicted in digital images, from stopping water to conveying the impression of speed. It also covers sports photography and shows how to capture continuous shots.

Covers

70 Stopping water

Water is one of the great substances for photography. It can take on different forms such as snow and ice; it can be static or moving; it can be used for reflections; it can take on different colors and textures (ripples); and it can be rendered in different ways using various photographic techniques. Overall it can be one of the most satisfying photographic subjects.

One photographic technique for water is showing how to freeze its motion. Not in the form of ice but rather a photographic freezing to create the appearance of the water having almost stopped in mid air. This can be done with any type of moving water, such as a stream, a waterfall, a hose or even a water slide.

Always keep your camera far away from water. If it gets wet it will almost certainly stop working. If this happens, dry it out completely before you try and use it again as this will increase the chances of it recovering fully.

The trick to making water freeze in an image is to use a fast shutter speed. To do this you will have to set your camera to shutter speed priority. This means that you can set the shutter speed and the camera will select an appropriate aperture. Select a shutter speed of at least 1/500th second, which should be fast enough to capture the water as it is falling but before it has moved too far. If there is enough light, and if your camera will allow it, you can use shutter speeds in the range of 1/2000th second. The image below was taken with a shutter speed of 1/1000th second, which resulted in a relatively wide aperture of f5.6. Due to the fast shutter speed the water is captured very quickly so that the individual drops are visible.

71 Blurring water

The opposite photographic technique to stopping water is making it blurred to convey a sense of motion. This can produce soft, almost cloud-like images that are very soothing and comforting. The best options for this are large waves, waterfalls and fast-moving streams or rivers.

For details about capturing images of water at night, see Tip 92.

When capturing images of blurred water you should use a tripod so that you can use shutter speeds that are slow enough to create the blurred effect. Start by setting the camera to shutter speed priority and use an initial shutter speed of 1/30th second to see the result. Then take the shot again several times, each time making the shutter speed one stop slower (the image below was taken with a shutter speed of 1/6th second). One drawback with this is that as the shutter speed gets slower, so more light enters the camera, even with the aperture at its narrowest setting. Depending on the amount of available light, there will probably come a point when the shutter speed is too slow resulting in the image being over-exposed, i.e. too much light entering the camera. Because of this, the best time to capture blurred water images is on an overcast day when the natural light is not too bright.

Once you have mastered capturing images of blurred water you may want to start actively searching out water scenes so that you can experiment further with this technique.

72

Capturing speed

Showing the impression of speed in a still image is obviously something of a challenge. By its very nature, digital photography is a static medium, but this is not to say that it is impossible to convey the idea of speed. This can be done for any fast moving object: vehicles, animals and people.

One way that the impression of speed is depicted in photography is to show the moving object against a blurred background. This serves to create the idea of speed by showing that the object is moving so quickly that the background cannot be caught in focus. The trick here is to ensure that the moving object is in sharper focus than the background and this is done by using a technique called panning.

A similar effect to panning is known as tilting. This is when the camera follows a vertically moving object (such as a rocket) rather than a horizontal one.

Panning works by following a moving object in the viewfinder or LCD panel of a camera and then capturing the image while the moving camera is still following the object. For instance, if a vehicle is moving from point A to point C, via point B, this can be used for the panning technique. Start following the vehicle at point A and capture the image at point B, but make sure the camera moves with the vehicle the whole way.

There are two important factors to remember when panning on a moving object. The first is the point of focus. If the vehicle is the same distance from you the whole time it is being followed by the camera, then you can focus when it first comes into view and keep this locked (keep the shutter release button held halfway down) until you take the shot. If the distance of the object varies during its journey, then you should pre-focus on a specific point, keep this locked, and capture the shot when the object is at this point. The second factor is to make sure the whole object is in the viewfinder or LCD panel when the image is captured. If you are at an event where you will only get a few chances to get it right (such as a motor sports event) then practice beforehand so as to perfect the technique.

Panning can be used on any moving object, such as the vehicle in the top image on the facing page or the child in the bottom image. If a person is involved, make sure that they are moving fast enough to create the blurred effect in the background.

73

Blurring speeding objects

reating a blurred effect for speeding objects is similar to capturing blurred images of water: a slow shutter speed is required to enable the speeding object to become blurred. However, since objects such as vehicles, and people, are usually faster than water the technique is slightly different.

When creating blurred effects for vehicles, animals or people there are two options. The first is to create an image that is universally blurred; the second is to have a blurred object over a sharp background. The image below shows the effect when the whole image is blurred. This is created by panning the camera on the speeding object, but not focusing. This results in the whole image being blurred, which creates a slightly surreal impression of speed.

The other way to capture blurred speeding objects is to use a slow shutter speed and, holding the camera still, let them move past the camera. The shutter speed should not be too slow, otherwise they would move through the frame before the shot was completed. The top image on the facing page was captured at a shutter speed of 1/60th second and the bottom one at 1/30th second. In both cases the shutter speed was just fast enough so that the camera could be hand-held without the need for a tripod.

To blur images of vehicles, a faster shutter speed can usually be used than for blurring images of people, since vehicles will probably be moving faster.

74

Continuous shooting

When dealing with shots involving motion it is not uncommon to wish that you could capture several shots in a row, to capture the action at split-second intervals. Traditionally, this type of functionality was only available on high-end cameras. However, it is now increasingly common to find a continuous shooting option on a wide range of digital cameras. If you want to be able to capture continuous shots then you will have to look for a camera with this specific function.

Continuous shooting mode can drain digital camera batteries a lot faster than taking individual shots.

Continuous shooting is measured in frames per second, i.e. how many shots the camera can take in this mode in one second. The lowest level will be about 3 frames per second, going up to approximately 8 frames per second for more expensive cameras. To capture continuous shots you have to select this option either from a button on the camera

In continuous mode the camera will keep capturing images until you take your finger off the shutter release button

body or from the camera's internal menu system. Once this has been done you use the continuous shooting mode in the same way as taking a single shot: half-depress the shutter release button to focus the image and then fully depress it to capture the shot. In continuous mode the camera will keep capturing images until you take your finger off the shutter release button.

In continuous shooting mode, the focus is locked for the first image and remains like this for any subsequent ones.

Continuous shooting can be used in any photographic situation but it is most effective in shots involving action such as sports shots. Sometimes the action is too fast to guarantee capturing a perfect image in a single shot and with continuous shooting your chances of getting the shot you want increase significantly. It is also good for producing a series of action images, as with the series of photographs on the facing page.

Continuous shooting can also be a good option for capturing portraits, particularly of children, who tend to move more during the photographic process. If you use continuous shooting then there is more chance of capturing an acceptable image even if the child is blinking, talking or moving.

75 Sports shots

Sport covers a multitude of activities, each of which provides the photographer with a rich source of potential material. The essential factor in sports photography is to capture the essence of a particular sporting event: the physical nature of a football game, the grace of an ice skater or the power and intensity of a weightlifter.

Since a lot of sporting activities involve motion, it is important to use a fast shutter speed to capture the majority of sports shots. If a digital camera has a Sports mode option, this will automatically use a shutter speed that is fast enough to freeze the action (as long as there is enough available light). In general, aim to use a shutter speed of 1/250th second or faster in sports shots where there is fast moving action. In some cases, such as catching a baseball coming off a bat, you may need a shutter speed of about 1/1000th second or faster.

For a lot of sports shots it is all about capturing the action and this means that you have to be reasonably close to the participants. For this type of photography it is essential to have a powerful zoom function on your camera and this is a case of "the bigger the better". Experiment by capturing an image of a sporting event with no zoom applied. Even if they look relatively close with the naked eye, the participants will look frustratingly small in the image. Next, try zooming in as much as possible to capture the action and, if possible, the expressions on the faces of the participants. If your camera has a continuous shooting mode (see previous Tip) this is an excellent option for sports photography: even the best photographers have problems capturing the split-second action in a fast-moving sporting event and continuous shooting enables you to capture several frames in very quick succession.

When performing sports photography, do not just concentrate on fast-moving action. Sports such as gymnastics offer the chance to capture grace and poise and it is also a good idea to capture some general shots, such as the venue and the expressions of other people in the crowd. Anything that helps to capture the essence of the event is worthwhile in this context.

Be prepared to take a lot of unsatisfactory images when you first start sports photography. Knowing when to take the shot is a skill that takes a bit of time to learn, but it can pay impressive dividends.

PROFESSIONALS

Professional sports photographers use very large zoom lenses with monopods to help keep them steady.

MOTION

144

Creating ghostly shadows

Trick photography has been around for as long as cameras themselves. With the advent of digital cameras and image editing software this has been taken to a level where we can no longer be sure that a digital image is a genuine, unadulterated original or not. But within digital cameras it is still possible to create original images with a trick element, without the need to resort to software wizardry. One of these tricks is the creation of ghostly shadows in an image.

If you are capturing images of groups of people at night be prepared for some of them to come and investigate what you are doing, hopefully in a friendly fashion.

To create effective shadows of people in an image you will need a tripod and a dark night. Set up the tripod near an area where there are a reasonable number of people. Try and ensure that the overall composition of the image is good too so that you do not have to rely solely on the people in the image. Then, set the camera to shutter speed priority mode and set the shutter speed to a minimum of 10 seconds (the longer the exposure time, the more shadows you will achieve). Once you have activated the shutter release button the people who pass the camera will be captured as shadowy outlines, as in the image below. Try and ensure that there are some people who are standing still, too, to give more solid-looking images. This technique can also be used for two people: get one to stand still and the other to move through the image to play the part of the ghost.

MOTION

145

Effects for motion

Even though there are techniques for showing the motion of objects it is sometimes useful to have a backup option. This is because capturing moving vehicles or people can be a bit hit-and-miss and in some cases you may only get one chance to catch the shot. If you miss it, it is a good idea to have an alternative.

One option for depicting motion is to create a digitally enhanced image with image editing software. This can be done by initially capturing an image of a static object against a suitable background. Once this image has been downloaded onto a computer it can then be edited using a program such as Photoshop, Photoshop Elements or Paint Shop Pro.

The first step in the editing process is to select the main subject. This can be done with one of the selection tools, such as the lasso tool, the polygonal lasso tool or the magnetic lasso tool. When this has been completed, invert the selection so that the whole of the background is selected. To create the impression of speed, apply a filter blur effect. The best one to use is motion blur as you can select a direction for this. Adjust the amount of blur so that it appears that the main subject is speeding past the background (see below). For added effect, if a car or similar vehicle is being used, select the wheels and add the same blurred effect to them.

COMPOSITION

How scenes are composed is crucial to the final image. This section shows how to make the most of the elements in a scene and gives you creative ideas for deliberately composing images rather than just capturing the first scene that presents itself.

Covers

Location, location, location

Occasionally great photographs are captured completely by chance – very much a case of just being in the right place at the right time. However, occurrences like this are few and far between and if you want to capture consistently good images a little bit of work and planning is required.

One of the most crucial elements of photography is location: i.e. where you are and where you then position yourself in relation to your chosen subject. In terms of location, you do not have to jet off to exotic parts of the world to find worthwhile subject matter (although travel can be one of the most prolific sources of photographic material). The important thing to remember about location is that you should be able to take good photographs wherever you are.

The first thing to do when you are assessing a location for photographic opportunities is to decide what type of shots you want to take. A good exercise is to select one theme (close-ups, landscapes, portraits etc.) and then shoot a selection of these types of shots for any given location. Before you start shooting you should get to know your location (always take your camera with you, though, in case a quality shot presents itself). If possible walk around your chosen location with a view to photographic opportunities. Also, look at the lighting and work out where the sun will rise and set so that you can make the most of the Golden Hour (see Tip 23). If you have a good knowledge of your location, and the points where you want to capture images, you will be able to spend more time taking pictures rather than worrying about finding the best vantage point.

Even when you have what seems like a perfect location it is always worth exploring different angles and points of view. This is particularly true of popular tourist spots: the point where most people congregate is probably not the best place from which to capture good photographs. Make a conscious effort to leave the crowds behind and find a point that offers the chance to capture something a bit more interesting than a standard holiday snapshot. This type of photography takes a bit more time but it will result in much more compelling images. Good locations are vital for photography but it is what you do when you get there that will make the difference in the final image.

When you are checking out any location make sure that you are allowed to take photographs there and always be careful around military installations and airports.

Timing, timing, timing

Just as location is important for image taking, so is timing. This involves the time of day at which you are capturing images and also the amount of time you spend when you are taking a shot: it is easy to rush picture taking but it is sometimes beneficial to spend time over one shot to ensure that it is the best you can achieve, rather than take several shots quickly, without any of them turning out perfectly.

The first issue with photographic timing is the actual time of day during which you are shooting. Sometimes you do not have any control over this but if you have the chance to capture images at times of your choosing then this opens up a variety of creative possibilities. As shown in Tip 23 the best light for photography in terms of richness of color and texture is approximately one hour after sunrise and one hour before sunset. Also, for night photography, the best time is frequently one hour after sunset as this is when there is still enough color in the sky (frequently a rich, dark purple) to give an extra dimension to night shots. Whenever you are going to take pictures, check the times of sunrise and sunset (particularly if you are in an unfamiliar location) and work out the position where the sun will rise and set. This will enable you to work out the best locations at certain times of the day. If you know the timing of the best light in the day you will then be able to make sure you are in position to utilize it for as long as possible.

Try and do as much work as possible before you get to a location as this will give you more time for taking pictures. Items such as sunset and sunrise times can easily be checked on the Internet for a variety of locations.

The second issue with timing covers the physical process of capturing images. Frequently in photographic situations it is all too easy to rush the image capturing process. This can be exaggerated if you are faced with an especially enticing scene: the tendency is to rattle off a lot of images quickly in order not to miss the shot. A better option is to take your time, check your camera settings, ensure you have the best composition, set up your camera on a tripod if necessary, focus accurately and then capture the image. Quality over quantity wins every time.

Sometimes just a few minutes can make all the difference to an image. Waiting for a cloud to move so that the sun comes out to illuminate your subject can turn an average image into a standout one. If you are aware of your surroundings you can time your picture taking accordingly.

80 Rule of thirds

As mentioned in Tip 36 an image can be improved by having the main subject away from the center of the image. This can give it a more natural appearance and make it look less posed. However, it is not just a case of positioning the subject anywhere out of the center of the image, which could result in an unbalanced picture. Instead imagine your image as a grid of 3 x 3 squares and position your subject at the intersection point of any of the grid lines or in one of the subsequent sectors (see below). This should provide you with an eye-catching and balanced composition.

This is known as the "rule of thirds" and it can be applied to give an image a completely different perspective. Always keep this in mind when you are capturing images and experiment with the subject in different areas of the rule of thirds grid. In the two images on the facing page the composition of the pictures has been altered considerably by moving the main subject to different points in the rule of thirds grid.

Sometimes the best shot is to have the main subject in the center of the frame, so always consider this as an option too.

Moving the horizon

A similar technique to the rule of thirds is that of moving the horizon. This is simply a case of repositioning the camera so that the horizon appears at different places in each shot. If you do this then you can have three shots with the horizon at the top, middle and bottom of the image. The three images on these two pages were captured from the same point and create different viewpoints by altering the position of the horizon. This can be achieved by moving the camera very slightly up or down between shots. Only a small adjustment is required to create dramatically different scenes from shot to shot.

Framing with existing elements

The first thing that many of us do with a pleasing photographic image is to put it in a frame to show it at its best. This is a normal reaction but it is also possible to use elements in scenes to act as frames within the image itself. This serves to emphasize part of an image and provides an extra artistic element to the picture.

When looking for items to use as frames within images the list is extensive: doorways, arches, branches, bridges, holes and pillars are just a few. The trick is to position yourself so that the frame is in the correct position and not obscuring a significant part of the image itself. The frame object should also be thought of as an important part of the image. It can be placed around the very border of the image or it can be a central part of the image in its own right. In the image below the branches act as a frame for the background but they are still an important element of the image. In the top image on the facing page the statue acts as a frame for the lamp behind it, but at this distance the statue is still the main object. In the bottom image on the facing page, a close-up of the statue serves to better frame the lamp and the depth of field highlights the distance between the two objects.

83 Finding focal points

The focal points in an image are nothing to do with getting objects in focus correctly (although this should be done as a matter of course). The term refers to the object, or area, that is given the most prominence in an image – the main focus of attention for the viewer.

In general, most images have one main focal point and you should always compose images with this in mind. There can certainly be additional focal points, which are of less importance but help to add to the effectiveness of the overall image. Sometimes there can be two main focal points, but this can be distracting, leading to confusion as the viewer does not know where to concentrate their attention between the two.

Focal points do not have to be single objects: in the case of a landscape, a whole mountain range could be the focal point. In the image on the left, the building is the main focal point, with the bushes in the foreground acting as a secondary focal point. In the image below, all of the water lilies are the main focal point even though they take up most of the image.

Framing with zoom

Most digital cameras have some form of zoom facility and this should always be considered when looking at the composition of an image. The impact and character of a scene can be changed dramatically through the use of zoom.

Zoom has the advantage of being able to pick out compositions that would not be apparent if a wide angle lens were used. The more that you zoom in on an image, the more detail you see. This can then be used to compose the image. (Even when zoom is used it is also good practice to capture some images with a wider angle lens, since these may depict the overall character of a scene.)

The image on the left was captured with a wide angle lens of approximately 20mm. While it is pleasant enough it does not have any great impact in terms of composition. The image on the right is of the same scene but taken with a zoom lens at 300mm. This brings the various elements of the image into play and the trees and bushes can now be used to frame the bridge and river.

COMPOSITION

85 Getting involved in the picture

An important element in taking better photographs is to start thinking like a photographer, rather than just someone who points a camera at a scene and presses the button. This does not mean that you have to have expensive photographic equipment: great images can be captured with any type of camera, particularly if you are prepared to make a bit of effort in finding good shots.

Some options for getting involved in an image are advisable, while others are not. For instance, it may be acceptable to wade into the middle of a shallow river, but not to walk into the middle of a busy road.

One mistake a lot of camera users make is to capture images from a single point, usually the one they arrive at first. For instance, dozens of tourists will capture the same images at the point where the tour bus stops. To get the best shots it is sometimes necessary to look around and find the best vantage point for capturing an image. One way to do this is to physically get involved in the picture, positioning yourself so that it looks as if you are virtually in the scene. This can involve getting into unusual positions, such as climbing a tree or lying down on the ground, but it can be worth it. The image below was captured by lying flat on a rock in the middle of the river, and gives the impression of actually being in the river itself. If you get involved in the scene when you are capturing it, the end result should have a more natural appearance.

Thinking creatively

You do not have to be faced with a stunning natural vista or a world-famous landmark to take effective and eye-catching images. With a little creative thinking anyone can capture worthwhile images in most locations and in most weather and lighting conditions. The trick is to think creatively and believe that you can capture images in any situation. Don't be daunted by the idea of creativity: anyone can be creative, it just takes a little practice and imagination.

One way to start thinking creatively is to look at as many different photographs as possible. Study books, magazines, advertisements and any other media that contain photographs. Analyze the style of the photographs, the composition, the angles at which the images are captured and the lighting. Once you have

Study books, magazines, advertisements and any other media that contain photographs

an understanding of the creative elements of the types of images you like then you can set about trying to replicate them. This does not mean that you should try and create an exact copy of the images you like – just use these techniques as a guide for your own picture taking. Concentrate on one area at a time, such as composition, and try to take an active role in framing images in the way you want and in a similar style to the types of images you enjoy. After a while it will become more natural to employ these techniques and the creative process will become more intuitive.

Another way to stretch your creativity is to choose an un-exotic location and then try and take as many effective images as possible. Try in your own garden or a local industrial site or building site. Remember, your shots do not have to be of sweeping landscapes or palm-fringed beaches to be creative. For instance, try experimenting with shots of textures (wood, metal, plastic) or patterns such as bricks or scaffolding. The more apparently mundane the location, the more creative you will be forced to be, but this could result in some unexpectedly effective images. Start thinking like a photographer and soon you will be capturing images like one too.

87 Still life

Still life images are perhaps more commonly associated with paintings but it is a subject that should not be overlooked for photographic images. In simple terms, a still life is an image of a collection of inanimate objects. These can be arranged in an artistic or a humorous way and the end result is frequently in the eye of the beholder.

Creating still life images can be an art in itself and it is sometimes easier to find still life scenes that other people have created and then use these in your images. Good areas to look at are businesses that are trying to attract people into their premises, as this is often done with eye-catching still life designs. Shops, restaurants, cafés and pubs often have still life displays near their doorways: it is usually better to look around areas with smaller, more specialized outlets rather than large malls or shopping centers. The image on the facing page was captured outside a café in France: the combination of fruit, lighting and background creates an evocative scene that captures the essence of the establishment.

Still life images can be captured in a wider context in addition to the objects themselves. For instance, a still life within a shop window shows that it is serving a specific purpose, i.e. trying to attract customers.

If you want to create your own still life images you will first have to create the still life itself. This may depend on your artistic ability but try and follow a few general rules. Base your still life scenes on single themes, such as food, art, sport or technology. This is not to say that you cannot have unconnected objects for emphasis but try and choose the majority of the items from the same general group. Then arrange the items so that they can all be viewed (or at least parts of them can). Keep smaller objects more towards the front and larger ones at the back and try to aim for an even composition, i.e. one in which nothing looks out of place. The element on which the still life is placed is also important: there is little point having a well-crafted still life that is on an incongruously shabby table. Treat every element in the still life as a crucial one.

The final thing to think about before you photograph the still life is the lighting. You may need to add extra lighting to illuminate different parts of the scene. If possible, make it portable so that you can position it as required in natural lighting.

SUBJECTS

Fruit, vegetables and flowers make excellent subjects for still life images and all three can be combined.

Waiting for the right shot

As with anything, luck plays its part in good photography. Sometimes a perfect image will just present itself in front of you. Unfortunately this is a rare event, but you can increase your chances of it by trying to be in the right place at the right time. Try planning the shot that you want to take and be in the correct position to take advantage of it when it comes along.

By definition, waiting for the right shot to come along can take time but it definitely pays to be patient and stay at a location for as long as you can. The image below is a good example of this. I was capturing images of car lights but decided to wait a bit longer, just in case something more interesting came along. After half an hour, a maintenance truck went past with several tail-lights on the back of its safety sign. The resultant image is slightly different from a standard tail-light one. This was a case of making my own luck through waiting long enough.

For some shots it can just be a case of waiting a few minutes until the sun comes from behind a cloud. The top image on the facing page was captured on what appeared to be an overcast day. However, I could see from the weather that the clouds were lifting. Sure enough, after 20 minutes the sun came out and I was able to capture the much more satisfying image at the bottom of the facing page. For a lot of photographic situations, it is worth trying to work out how the scene will look in an hour or two and then act accordingly.

If you are waiting for a specific shot, do not give up just because you do not capture it first time. Go back at the next available opportunity and try again: some of the most satisfying images are those that require a bit of work.

89 Photo essays

Some photographic locations offer the chance for one single, stunning image. However, in most cases, there are numerous opportunities for capturing a variety of images. Even if you cannot immediately see the chance for different images it is always worthwhile looking around a location to see if you can capture a range of shots. Once you have perfected this you should be able to create a photo essay in almost any situation. This is a collection of images that together give a sense of the character of a location.

Think "themes" when you are in a photographic location, rather than just individual shots. Find groups of linked subjects and capture these in a variety of situations.

Wherever you are with your camera try and think of the different types of shots that are available. For instance, if you are on holiday on the beach you may take some family shots of people playing in the sand. But then have a look at the sea and the waves and try to capture some artistic shots by stopping the water or giving it the appearance of motion. Then take a walk along the beach and look in rock pools for any signs of life. Also, take some texture shots of the rocks and plants themselves. Finally, at the end of the day capture some social shots of people leaving the beach, to contrast with the action and enjoyment of earlier in the day. Look at the obvious and then try and enhance this with as many different types of shots as possible. The end result will create a much more interesting collection.

The collection of images on the following pages was captured at Barcelona Harbour, to try and show all of the different characteristics of this area.

UNUSUAL CONDITIONS

Not all photographs are taken on bright, sunny days. This section contains tips for capturing images in a variety of lighting and weather conditions. This includes a number of night photography situations as well as shooting in the snow and the rain. It also covers tips for capturing images of animals and food, and for taking product shots.

90 Fireworks

The combination of color, patterns and movement is a captivating one in photographs and this is rarely better displayed than through fireworks. Fireworks displays are increasingly common, particularly on major holidays such as national holidays, Thanksgiving and New Year. For photography, organized displays are best as they usually go on for the longest time and have the best range of fireworks (and since you do not have to organize anything you can concentrate on capturing images rather than setting off pyrotechnics).

If you are going to be capturing fireworks images at an organized display, try and arrive early so that you can get to the best location. Since you will be shooting at night, you will need a tripod to keep the camera steady. Although you will be operating in low-level lighting, fireworks photography can include a variety of different shutter speeds. Experiment with a fast shutter speed (approximately 1/60th or 1/125th second) to see if you can capture individual fireworks going off. The reason that a relatively fast speed can be used at night is that the fireworks themselves give off enough light for some interesting effects to be created.

At an organized display, try and arrive early so that you can get to the best location

Generally, slightly slower shutter speeds will create a more artistic effect and capture the sense of both color and motion. The images on the facing page were captured with a shutter speed of 1/4 second, which captures the fireworks as they explode and move through the sky.

SPARKLERS

Sparklers are another option for fireworks images as these tend to leave interesting trails of light.

Another way of capturing fireworks is to use a long exposure by setting the shutter speed to between five and ten seconds. This will enable you to capture several exploding fireworks in the same shot and it is very effective with a wide angle lens from distance.

Car tails

I mages of car tail-lights at night are a very satisfying exercise for night photography. The colored streaks that are created convey a sense of motion while producing images that have a surreal quality about them.

The more cars that have passed through an exposure, the more streaks there will be in the image.

When trying to capture car tail-lights at night, select a location where you know there will be enough cars passing by. Depending on the time of year, you may be able to capture images during the rush hour, if the sun has gone down already. Make sure you are not physically on the road and use a tripod to keep the camera steady since you will be using a very slow shutter speed.

The trick with car tail-lights is to have a long enough exposure so that the vehicles have time to pass through the whole of the frame, causing the colored streaks to go into the distance. In the image below, the aperture was set to f16 to get as large a depth of field (as much of the image in focus) as possible. The shutter speed was set to 10 seconds so that the lights were caught throughout the image, but the moving vehicles were not visible as they were moving too quickly to be captured during this length of exposure. If cars are moving away from the camera the lights will be red and if they are moving towards the camera the lights will be white.

Water at night

Tips 70 and 71 showed how different photographic effects can be achieved when capturing images of water. The photographic possibilities of water are increased once night falls and the opportunities for capturing images of water in the dark arise.

The crucial factor when capturing images of water at night is the use of a tripod. Due to the low levels of light, a shutter speed of several seconds will be required to allow enough light to enter the camera. If a tripod is not used the whole image will be blurred.

The use of a slow shutter speed has a significant impact on the appearance of the water in the final image. Since the water is still moving while the shutter is open this will create a blurred effect that takes on a soft, cottonwool-like appearance. As long as there is some source of light this technique can create some stunningly atmospheric images. The image below was taken with an aperture of f8 and shutter speed of 30 seconds. The scene was dimly lit by the moon, which provided enough light to give the moving water a bluish tinge. The image overleaf was captured at f11 with a shutter speed of 10 seconds. This is because the lighting from the bridge provided more illumination so the shutter speed could be shorter than in the image below.

UNUSUAL CONDITIONS

171

Illuminating buildings

Shots of buildings during the day can be very satisfying and effective, but there is something about buildings at night that can give them a more glamorous and exciting appearance. In cities and towns around the world there are buildings that are illuminated at night and this presents them in an ideal condition for photography.

When capturing buildings at night, select ones that have some form of artificial lighting to illuminate them. This will give them the required lighting to make them stand out against their background. Another thing to remember with images of buildings at night is not to use the flash. This is because most flash units on digital cameras are not powerful enough to illuminate something as large as a building and they will only light up a small part of the foreground instead. (Flash can be used, but only if you are taking a close-up of one specific part of a building.)

For images of buildings at night a tripod is essential. Because of the low levels of light, a slow shutter speed will be required so a tripod will be needed to keep the camera steady. As with any type

Always bracket exposures when capturing buildings at night (or any night shots). This involves using exposure compensation either one or two stops above or below the exposure settings selected by the camera.

of building image, try and capture the image from a spot where you can include the whole building and also foreground objects, if there are any. The top image on the facing page was captured with a shutter speed of two

A slow shutter speed will be required so a tripod will be needed to keep the camera steady

seconds in order to get enough light into the camera. Since the building was well illuminated, the shutter speed did not have to be any slower than this. The image is improved by the laser show that was taking place from the roof and it is always worth investigating if there are any buildings with light shows near where you are (a lot of major cities around the world have this type of event).

Details of buildings can also be captured at night. These are frequently illuminated by individual spotlights, as with the bottom image on the facing page. This image required a shutter speed of only one second since there was a reasonable amount of light from the spotlights, but at this length of exposure a tripod is still definitely needed.

94 Cityscapes at night

When night falls this should not be the time to pack cameras away. In fact the opposite is true as this can be the time to capture stunning images. One popular option is cityscapes at night, when the buildings are illuminated and the street lights provide an additional source of light. If you are planning to do this, take some time out during the day to find potential locations and compositions as this will save you a lot of time and effort when it gets dark.

In the same way that the best light for daytime photography occurs an hour after sunrise and an hour before sunset, so the best time for night photography can be one hour after sunset. This produces a dusky light that still has some color in the sky from the reflected sun. This is known as an after-light and is frequently a dark purple in color, which can provide rich backdrops for cityscapes.

A group of buildings can convey the character of a city

One option when capturing cityscapes is to concentrate on a group of buildings. This can convey the character of a city and groups of skyscrapers are ideal for this, as in the top image on the facing page, which shows the Las Vegas depiction of New York skyscrapers. For this type of shot, use a wide angle lens (or a zoom lens with the zoom fully retracted) and a slow shutter speed. In this example, a shutter speed of 8 seconds was used, with the camera on a tripod.

Another option for cityscapes at night is to find a location above the city that serves to capture its overall character, as shown in the bottom image on the facing page. To do this you may have to climb a nearby hill or try and find a tall building that you can go up during the evening. This type of shot will probably take a bit of hard work as far as finding a location is concerned, but it should be worth it. Again, use a tripod and a slow shutter speed: the bottom image on the facing page was taken with a narrow aperture (f16) to create a large depth of field and a shutter speed of 30 seconds.

BE CAREFUL

Take care when photographing cities at night and try not to look too conspicuous.

95 Single lights in the dark

If you capture traffic lights with a long exposure (approximately 5 seconds) then there is a chance of capturing all three lights together. Try and work out the sequence of the lights first, and how long each one remains illuminated for.

I f you are taking shots at night without a flash this does not necessarily mean that you need a tripod and a slow shutter speed in order to allow enough light to enter into the camera. A different option is to capture images of bright lights against a dark background. This can produce very striking photographs and it is possible to create images like this without a tripod. This technique can be used very effectively for items such as street lights and traffic lights.

The image below was captured by first locking the exposure on one of the lights in the image (see Tip 30 for details about exposure lock). This gave a shutter speed of 1/60th second (fast enough to hand-hold the camera). Then, the scene was recomposed with the shutter release button still held down to maintain the exposure lock. The image was then captured and the relatively fast shutter speed ensured that the background was very under-exposed, thus rendering it black, adding to the effectiveness of the image with the bright lights.

Product shots

There are some forms of photography that are very specialized and use similarly specialized equipment. One of these is the product shot. These are the types of images in magazines and pamphlets that are used to display products at their best. Although a lot of these images look as if they would be easy to capture, this is not always the case.

Even if you do not have to take product shots as part of your working life, there will probably be occasions when you will need to capture images of inanimate objects for things like newsletters or school projects.

The main problem with capturing images of individual objects is the glare or reflection that comes from them. In any form of light most objects will produce some form of glare or reflection. One option is to use flash, but this too can reflect off the object, causing a white flare in the image. If you have an external flash unit, the flash can be bounced off a ceiling or a wall to reduce or eliminate the glare effect. Another option is to use a lamp as the light source instead of the flash.

The main problem with capturing images of individual objects is glare or reflection

If you are capturing a product shot with natural light, try doing this early in the morning and placing the object on a white sheet next to an open window. Capture images from different angles to see which one produces the best result in terms of reflection and glare, or lack of them.

The professional answer to the problem of product shots is a white dome called a Cloud Dome. This has an attachment for the camera and creates an even lighting source that eliminates reflection.

BACKGROUNDS

White or colored sheets can be used to remove a cluttered or messy background. This gives more emphasis to the product itself rather than the background.

UNUSUAL CONDITIONS

Snow scenes

Initially, it may seem that images of snow are simple to capture: you compose the scene and then snap away to create numerous winter scenes. This is true to a certain extent, but the problem is that, unless some corrective action is taken, the images will appear with gray snow, rather than the more traditional white. This is to do with how a digital camera measures light.

By default, internal light meters in digital cameras work by seeing everything as a "neutral gray". This means that they work out the correct light in a scene by calculating the amount of light reflected back to the camera as if all subjects were a neutral gray color. This is because neutral gray reflects approximately 18% of the light that hits it and this is the optimal level for measuring light in most photographic scenes. This is also known as 18% reflectance.

When capturing images of snow, or predominantly black scenes, use a gray card to take a meter reading to avoid the problems of 18% reflectance. The reading can be made from the card and this will ensure that the snow appears white. Gray cards can be purchased from most photographic retailers.

The problem with 18% reflectance and neutral gray is when it comes in contact with pure black or white. This is because they reflect either a lot less or a lot more light: black reflects approximately 9% of light and white reflects approximately 36% of light. What this means for capturing snow is that the camera will render it as 18% reflectance rather than 36%, which means the snow will appear as a neutral gray rather than white.

There are two options for capturing genuine white snow. One way is to take a normal metering reading and then use exposure compensation (see Tip 34 for details) to add more light into the scene (one or two stops of exposure compensation is enough). Another option is to take a light meter reading from a non-white area of the scene. This will create a correct exposure and the scene can then be recomposed and captured. In the top image on the facing page the light meter reading was taken from the snow, resulting in an image with a bluish gray tinge. In the middle image the exposure was taken from the blue sky just above the mountain. This ensured that the exposure would be correct for the whole image once the scene was recomposed.

Once the metering for snow scenes has been mastered you can then concentrate on the composition. This can involve a scene of fresh snow, in which case it is always advisable to include at least one other object for interest. In some cases, as in the bottom image on the facing page, it sometimes pays to get out and about as the snow is falling as this can produce dramatic images. However, make sure you keep the camera dry.

98 Let it rain

Rain is one weather condition that leads a lot of photographers to pack their cameras away and go and do something else instead. However, rainy days can be excellent for capturing evocative landscapes or as social comment shots of events that have been ruined due to the rain, e.g. an empty fairground on a rainy day.

The most important factor when shooting in the rain is to keep the camera dry. The best option is probably a dedicated waterproof camera bag. This is a bag that fits around the camera with a hole at the front for the lens. Some waterproof bags also have enough room at the back to cover the photographer's head while they are looking through the viewfinder or LCD panel. Another option is to create a home-made version of a waterproof bag. This can just be a plastic bag that is wrapped around the camera with a hole cut out for the lens. If you use this option, get your hands on a relatively strong plastic bag and make sure it does not have any additional holes in it.

When you are out shooting in the rain, try and find somewhere sheltered for capturing your images. This is because even if your camera is protected the lens will get rain spots on it if you are in an uncovered location. A tripod is also a good idea because the light levels will be a lot lower than on a sunny day and so you may require a slow shutter speed in order to capture rainy scenes.

If you do not want to physically go out in the rain it is still possible to capture images of rain. Shots through a rain-covered window are excellent for highlighting a sense of boredom or isolation caused by a rainy day, as with the image on this page. To achieve this, make sure that you focus on the raindrops on the window rather than the background. Using a manual focus facility, if you have one, would be a good way to do this.

If you are capturing images in the rain and there is lightning in the area, abandon the photography and get inside somewhere.

Capturing food

Food is another area that occupies a specialized niche in the professional market, but there is no reason why anyone with a digital camera cannot take impressive images of food and food-related items.

When dealing with food try to capture the essence of a particular type of food: the rich texture of chocolate by using a close-up shot, the freshness of an apple by cutting into it and showing the juice lying on the skin, or the size of a hot dog by photographing it length-on and at a low angle so that it fills the frame.

Try and create a sense of the dining experience rather than just the food on its own

It is also important to make an entire food scene as enticing as possible. If you are photographing a Thanksgiving Dinner for instance, include items such as the table setting, candles and flowers so that an overall ambience can be created. Try and create a sense of the dining experience rather than just the food on its own.

One valuable trick when capturing images of food is to do it when it is cold. This means that there will be no steam to cloud up the camera lens. Instead, try covering items with oil, or even wax, to give them that glistening appearance as if they are just out of the oven. This is how a lot of professional food shots are captured.

If you do capture food as it is being prepared, be careful not to get too close to saucepans and frying pans. This is because water or fat could splash onto the camera lens and spoil the shot, and potentially the camera too. Keep your distance and use a zoom lens to make the items look closer.

SPRAY IT ON

Fruit and vegetables can look a lot more enticing with water sprayed on them. This conveys a feeling of freshness, as if the produce has been picked in the early morning dew.

A common maxim in the cinema is "never work with animals or children," but it is not necessarily one that is true in digital photography. Certainly, it can take a bit more care and attention, and patience, to capture good images of children and animals, but the results can be very rewarding.

When capturing images of animals there are two main ways to go about it: either in the wild or in some form of confinement such as zoos, agricultural shows or wildlife parks. In the wild, it is a lot harder to get good pictures and you will need a good zoom facility and a lot of patience. Rather than chasing after animals, the best way to operate in the wild is to select a spot (and preferably use some form of hide or shelter) and then let the animals come to you. Depending on the type of wildlife this could take several hours but it is worth remembering that most stunning images of wildlife have probably taken days, or even weeks, to capture. It is rarely just a case of turning up, snapping away for a few minutes and then going home.

For animals in some form of captivity the photographer's job is made easier, if only because you know where the animals are going to be. When you are capturing images in these types of conditions it is also worth being patient so that you get the best possible shots. Try and avoid too much foreground or background detail that reveals your location. Try for images that show the character of the animals, like the one below and the top one on the facing page, or that show them in their natural environment, as in the bottom image on the facing page.

Do not get too close to wild animals, in case they become distressed or violent towards you. Instead, use as large a zoom lens as possible.

Creating "zoomed" images

Zoomed images can also be used for people, to create a sense of action and speed.

A lot of special photographic effects can be created through the use of image editing software. However, it is still possible for photographers to create some effects of their own while images are being captured. One of these is the effect of creating a "zoomed" image (see the example below).

In this context a zoomed image is one in which the zoom on the camera is moved as the shot is being captured. The easiest way to do this is with a digital SLR camera and a zoom lens of at least 18–70mm. With compact digital cameras that have a facility for adding lens attachments a similar effect could be achieved.

To create a zoomed image the camera has to be on a tripod, since a slow shutter speed will be used. Select an interesting subject and frame it in the middle of the viewfinder. Set the camera to shutter speed priority and select a shutter speed of at least 1/2 second. Focus the image and press the shutter release button. Simultaneously, zoom the lens from its longest focal length to its shortest (this is why a long shutter speed is required, to allow you enough time to zoom the lens). It will probably take a few attempts to get the timing right and you should try different shutter speeds to see how this affects the image. Also, try zooming from the shortest focal length to the longest to see the type of image that this produces.

INDEX